Fantastic facts

about

Fiendish things

by

S.L. Davis

WARNING

This book is written in a 'tongue in cheek', story-telling style. Nevertheless, it contains factual information that some will consider inhumane, frightening or abhorrent. If reading such information will upset you, please do not proceed.

Contents

Introduction.

They say that truth is stranger than fiction, but in the case of fiendish things, it's also just as terrifying. From ancient legends to modern-day sightings, this book delves into the dark and mysterious realm of the unknown, exploring the creatures and entities that have captured our imaginations for centuries. But be warned, reader: the contents of these pages are not for the faint of heart. Proceed with caution and an open mind, for the fiendish things that lie within will test your understanding of what is real and what is not.

Throughout history, humanity has been fascinated by the unknown, the inexplicable, and the fiendish. From myths and legends and unexplained sightings to our own horrible history, we have always sought to understand the mysteries of the world around us; the whys and wherefores. And among these mysteries, none are as fascinating and terrifying as the fiendish things that lurk in the shadows.

In my opinion, there is nothing wrong with being fascinated by the 'dark side'. As long as your own moral compass is strong and you empathise with others, you will not become 'bad' merely by reading about bad things. And most of us are fascinated to some extent by the grim and grisly, so you are in good company. You only have to look at the popularity of writers Stephen King, Dean Koontz or Shirley Jackson; or films like 'Alien', 'Poltergeist' or 'The Babadook'.

This book explores different aspects of the dark side – from bloodthirsty monsters, malevolent spirits, and otherworldly beings, to the fiendish happenings and things of the world. It examines the history, lore, and beliefs surrounding the fiendish and delves into various theories and explanations that have been put forth. Whether you're a skeptic or a believer, this book offers a thought-provoking examination of things that have captivated our minds for centuries.

But this is your *final warning* dear reader: the contents of these pages are not for the squeamish or faint-hearted. They will challenge your understanding of reality, make you wonder at the depth of human depravity, and may even make you question what you thought you knew about the world. They may haunt your mind for long after you cease reading. So if you decide to proceed, do so with caution my friend, and be prepared for a journey into the unknown, as we explore the dark and mysterious realm of the *fiendish things*.

Things that go bump in the night.
(Ghosts, vampires and more   )

The things that go bump in the night are the stuff of nightmares – the things that make us afraid to close our eyes and drift off to sleep. They're the monsters under the bed, the ghosts in the closet, the demons in our heads. They're the things that we can't quite explain, the things that we can't quite see. But we can certainly feel them in our fast-beating heart.

It could be the creak of a floorboard, the rustle of a tree branch against the window, the whispering of the wind through the cracks in the walls. It could be the memory of a past trauma, the fear of the unknown, or the dread of what's to come. The things that go bump in the night are different for all of us, but one thing is for sure: they're the things that keep us up at night, that make us question our own sanity. Did I see that? Did I hear that scream? *Well? Did you?*

But that's the beauty of it all, isn't it? The fear, the uncertainty, the not knowing. It's what makes life worth living, what makes stories worth telling. Because without the things that go bump in the night, where's the thrill? Where's the excitement of not knowing what's around the next corner? So go ahead, close your eyes and let the bumps in the night take you on a wild ride, as we try to decipher fact from fiction.

GHOSTS

Ghosts are the echoes of the past, the lingering remnants of lives once lived. They are the whispers in the dark, a cold spot in the room. They remind us that death may not be the end; that there are some things that science and reason can't explain. They remind us of our own mortality, of the loved ones we have lost, and of the things we have left undone. Perhaps they linger, waiting for us to join them in the great beyond.

But maybe the most terrifying thing about ghosts is that they are not just confined to the past. They can be found in the present, too, in the haunted houses and the cursed objects; in the memories that we can't shake; in the nightmares we can't escape. They remind us that death is always lurking, watching… and biding its time.

So, do they exist? Some say they are nothing more than the product of our fevered imaginations, while others claim to have had first-hand encounters with the paranormal. Let's have a look at some claimed encounters:

The Flying Dutchman, a ghost ship said to sail the seas forever, was first spotted by sailors off the coast of South Africa in the 17th century. The ship, said to be captained by a man who made a deal with the devil to avoid death, is doomed to sail the seas for eternity.

Another famous ghost sighting is the spectre of Anne Boleyn, the second wife of King Henry VIII. Executed in 1536 on charges of treason and adultery, her ghost is said to have been seen in the Tower of London, where she was imprisoned and executed.

Deep in the heart of Norfolk, England lies a country house steeped in mystery and haunted by the ghost of a woman wronged. Raynham Hall was her prison and her legacy. The Brown Lady, as she's known, was once a living, breathing woman named Lady Dorothy Townshend. She was the wife of Charles Townshend, a man who discovered her infidelity and locked her away in the house where she eventually died. But death was not the end for her. Her spirit remains trapped within the walls so it's said, forever seeking redemption and revenge. In 1936, a photographer captured an image of her as she descended the stairs, a ghostly figure dressed in brown, forever immortalized in one of the most famous ghost photographs of all time. Many have claimed to have seen her, from Townshend family members to servants and visitors, but none have been able to free her from her prison. Her story serves as a reminder of the eternal power of love and betrayal; and those who dare to enter Raynham Hall may well feel the brown lady's presence.

I could go on with many other claimed ghost sightings, but no book would be long enough. The existence of ghosts is a tantalising mystery. The possibility of their existence adds a certain frisson of fear to our everyday lives, a reminder that there are things beyond our understanding and control. For you, whether they really exist or not may be down to how much you want to believe. But the fact is, I'm sorry to say, there is no scientific evidence to support the existence of the supernatural, which is defined as entities, powers or events that cannot be explained by natural laws. Many supernatural beliefs are based on faith, personal experiences, and cultural or historical traditions, rather than on scientific evidence.

Scientists, (those men and women in white coats and glasses, with bald and shiny heads or white cotton skull caps) have investigated many claims of the supernatural, including ghosts, but there is no consistent evidence to support their existence. (The ghosts that is – not the scientists.) Studies on psychic abilities have been largely inconclusive, and many have been debunked as the result of fraudulent or mistaken claims. Also, some supernatural beliefs can be explained by natural causes, such as hallucinations, misinterpretations of natural events, or psychological factors.

However, it's important to recognise that science is a process of investigation and discovery and it is always possible that fresh evidence could emerge. And remember, the lack of scientific evidence supporting the existence of ghosts does not prove that they don't exist. Personally, I know a few reliable and truthful people who claim to have seen or heard ghosts. And between you and me… I believe them.

POLTERGEISTS

Poltergeists are the violent or agitated ghosts or spirits that are believed to cause physical disturbances, such as loud noises and objects moving on their own. The word "poltergeist" comes from the German words "poltern," meaning "to make noise," and "geist," meaning "ghost."

The phenomenon of poltergeist activity has been reported for centuries, with some of the earliest known accounts dating back to ancient Greece and Rome. In many cases, poltergeist activity is said to occur in a specific location, such as a house or a building, and is often associated with a particular person, such as a teenager going through puberty.

Some experts believe that poltergeist activity is caused by the subconscious mind of the person with whom the activity is associated, rather than an actual ghost or spirit. This theory is known as "recurrent spontaneous psychokinesis" and suggests that the individual's mind is able to unconsciously manipulate objects in their environment. However, others argue that poltergeist activity is truly supernatural in nature and caused by the spirits of the dead.

Poltergeists, like ghosts, are not a scientifically proven phenomenon. And many of the events that are reported as poltergeist activity can be explained by more prosaic causes such as natural phenomena, hoaxes, and misperceptions.

However, there have been several well-known reported cases of alleged poltergeist activity throughout history. One of the most famous is the Enfield Poltergeist case, which occurred in a council house in Enfield, England in the late 1970s. The activity was reported by two young sisters and included objects moving on their own, strange noises, and the girls' beds shaking. The case received widespread media attention and was investigated by both police and paranormal researchers.

Another famous case is the Amityville Horror, which took place in a house in Amityville, New York in the 1970s. The family who lived there claimed to have experienced a range of strange occurrences, such as doors and windows opening and closing on their own, strange noises, and objects moving on their own. The case was later made into a book and a film.

The Rosenheim Poltergeist case of 1967 in a law firm in Rosenheim, Germany is another famous case, where objects moved by themselves, phones rang without anyone on the other end, and even the lights were turned on and off by an unseen force.

You will need to make your own mind up my friend, but like ghosts, the lack of scientific evidence supporting the existence of poltergeists does not prove that they don't exist.

DEMONS

Demons are supernatural beings that have been feared for centuries. They are often portrayed as malevolent entities that seek to harm humans and spread chaos and destruction. But what exactly are demons, and where do they come from?

In many cultures, demons are believed to be fallen angels or evil spirits that have rebelled against the divine order: powerful entities that can possess humans and cause them to do terrible things. However, these beliefs are rooted in religion and mythology. There is no scientific evidence to support the existence of demons.

Despite this, demons have remained a popular topic in horror movies, books, and TV shows. They are often depicted as having frightening appearances, such as red skin, horns, and glowing eyes. They may also be shown possessing human bodies and causing them to act in violent and disturbing ways.

Whether you believe in the existence of demons or not, they remain an intriguing aspect of human culture and mythology. And maybe one day we'll discover the truth about these mysterious entities.

WEREWOLVES

Werewolves, the howling, hairy beasts of the full moon, also known as lycanthropes, are creatures from folklore that are said to have the ability to shape shift into a wolf or wolf-like creature. The concept of werewolves has been present in many cultures throughout history, and the beliefs and legends surrounding them have varied.

The most common belief about werewolves is that they are humans who can transform into wolves, either voluntarily or involuntarily, often during a full moon. In many legends, the transformation is said to be caused by a curse or a bite from another werewolf. In some cultures, werewolves were said to be evil creatures who hunted and killed humans, while in others they were seen as powerful protectors of the wild.

In recent years, the werewolf has been popularised in films, books, and on TV. But there is no scientific evidence to support the existence of werewolves, and the beliefs surrounding them are considered to be mythological and superstitious in nature.

There have been some individuals throughout history who have claimed to be werewolves or to have the ability to shape-shift into a wolf-like creature.

One of the most famous cases is the trial of Peter Stumpp, a German farmer who was accused of being a werewolf in the 16th century. He was said to have confessed to having made a pact with the devil

9

and to have killed and eaten several children and
pregnant women. He was found guilty, tortured and
executed. However, there is no known evidence to
back up the claims made, and it is likely that the
accusations were based on superstition and fear of
witchcraft.

Another reported case is the Beast of
Gévaudan, a large wolf-like creature that was said to
have attacked and killed people in the Gévaudan
province of France in the 18th century. The creature
was never captured, and so it is thought likely that the
attacks were caused by a pack of wolves rather than a
werewolf.

There is no evidence that any of these
individuals were actually werewolves, and the claims
are not considered credible by the scientific
community. But that doesn't prove Werewolves don't
exist, does it?

VAMPIRES

Vampires, those immortal bloodsuckers of legend,
have always been a source of fascination. The idea of
a creature that lives forever, yet is forever cursed to
live off the blood of the living, is a powerful one. It
taps into our deepest fears and desires, the fear of
death and the desire for immortality.

Vampires have appeared in fiction for
centuries, from the classic vampire Count Dracula to
the more modern, romantic vampire of Twilight. But
regardless of the specific iteration, the core of the
vampire remains the same: a being that exists in the
darkness, forever searching for its next bloody drink.
And yet, despite the monstrous nature of their

existence, we can't help but be drawn to them, to the idea of eternal life and the allure of the forbidden.

But let us not forget, these creatures are dangerous, and should not be trifled with. They may be seductive, but they are deadly. The vampire is a reminder of the darkness that lurks in the shadows, waiting to consume us, the stuff of nightmares and folklore, myths and legends. But do they exist in the real world? There is no scientific evidence to support the existence of these bloodsucking fiends. But does that mean they're not real? The vampire legend is a powerful thing, and it taps into our deepest fears and desires.

The concept of vampires has been present in many cultures throughout history, and the beliefs and legends surrounding them have varied. In most common folklore, vampires are often depicted as undead beings who rise from the grave to feed on the blood of the living, usually at night. They are often portrayed as having supernatural powers such as immortality, the ability to shape-shift, and the power to control the minds of others.

The vampire legends have been popularised in literature, the most famous book of all being Bram Stoker's 1897 novel 'Dracula'. In the past, accusations of vampirism were often made against individuals who were thought to be witches or other supernatural beings. In some cases, accusations of vampirism were also made against people who were believed to have died and risen from the dead.

In the 18th and 19th centuries, there were several vampire scares in Eastern Europe, where villagers would dig up the graves of their deceased loved ones, to check if they had become 'undead'. If the corpse was deemed to be a vampire, the villagers would burn, stake or behead the corpse, in order to prevent it from rising again.

There have been many different beliefs and practices throughout history that were thought to keep vampires away. These have varied depending on the culture and time period in which they were practiced. Some of the most common methods believed to protect against vampires include:

Garlic: Garlic was often believed to be a powerful repellent against vampires, and it was common to hang cloves of garlic in doorways, windows, or around the neck to ward off vampires.

Holy symbols: Crosses, religious medals and other holy symbols were believed to repel vampires, as vampires were unable to cross over them.

Stakes: It was believed that driving a wooden stake through the heart of a vampire would kill it.

Fire: Fire was also believed to be a powerful weapon against vampires, as it was thought that they would be unable to survive being burned.

Sunlight: Many vampire legends state that vampires cannot survive in sunlight, so being in the sun was considered a way to protect oneself from a vampire's attack.

Exorcism: In some cultures, exorcism was performed to drive away evil spirits, including supposed vampires.

Salt and iron: These elements were also believed to have protective properties and were placed in doorways, windows and graves to keep vampires away.

The belief that vampires cannot be seen in mirrors is a common one in vampire folklore and literature. According to this belief, a vampire does not have a reflection and therefore cannot be seen in a mirror. This idea is said to be linked to the vampire's lack of a soul, which is often associated with the vampire's undead status.

However, like ghosts, there is no scientific evidence to support the existence of vampires. But, (yes, you've guessed it!) this does not prove they don't exist. So, my friend – will you be hanging up garlic at your window tonight, before the dark and dangerous midnight hour?

ZOMBIES

They shuffle through the night, the living dead, driven by an insatiable hunger for human flesh. Zombies, once just a figment of our imagination, have now taken on a life of their own in popular culture. The origins of these flesh-eaters are many. Some say they're the result of voodoo curses, others claim they're the aftermath of radiation. They may be the product of a viral outbreak, spreading like wildfire through bites and contact with bodily fluids.

But what do these monsters truly represent? Some say they're a metaphor for consumerism, a commentary on our society's never-ending thirst for more. Others argue they're a warning of the dangers of viral outbreaks and the fragility of our modern world. But they may represent something even more terrifying - a reminder of our own mortality, a physical manifestation of the dead still walking.

The first zombie film, White Zombie, was released in 1932. It was a low-budget, independent film, but it was a hit among the audiences, and the start of a new era. The story followed a man who is turned into a zombie by a voodoo master and it was the first time that we saw the walking dead on the big screen.

But it was George A. Romero's Night of the Living Dead that truly cemented the zombie genre in popular culture. Released in 1968, it was a gritty, low-budget film that depicted the zombie as reanimated corpses, driven by a relentless hunger for human flesh. It truly captured the horror of the living dead and was a major influence on the genre for years to come. It will always be remembered as a classic of the genre.

But do they really exist? Some believe they're nothing more than the stuff of fiction, the product of overactive imaginations and a love for horror. Others argue that they're all too real, lurking just beyond the fringes of our understanding, waiting to rise up and devour us all. They exist in the pages of books, in the minds of those who read them, and in the hearts of those who fear them – but as for the walking dead, risen from the grave to feast on the living? I'm afraid that's the stuff of fiction, a nightmare conjured up by our own minds. There is no scientific evidence to prove their existence. But that doesn't mean they're not real, in some sense, for the fear that they instil in us is very real, and the threat they represent, even if it's not physical, is still there if it's in our minds. And if they exist in our heads and hearts, that's more than enough to keep us up at night.

The company we keep.

(Parasites, fearsome creatures and creepy-crawlies.)

The human body is a breeding ground for parasites, those insidious little buggers that lurk in the shadows, waiting to take up residence in unsuspecting hosts. They come in all shapes and sizes, from the tiny pinworm to the blood-thirsty malaria-carrying mosquito to the vampire bat. And once they've taken up residence, or just taken what they crave, they can cause all manner of trouble.

The mere thought of parasites crawling and wriggling inside of us is enough to make the flesh crawl. They can cause all sorts of unpleasant symptoms, from the itchy rash of lice to the fever and chills of malaria. They can rob us of our health and even our lives.

But perhaps the most terrifying thing about these parasites is that they hide in plain sight. They're everywhere, lurking in the food we eat, the water we drink, even the people we touch. But it's not only parasites that can harm us, is it? There's creepy crawlies that slither, burrow, and walk-up walls — and there's big creatures, too, that can bite, sting or rip us apart. But none, my friend— none are as lethal as humans. So don't have nightmares as we look at the fiendish creatures, because they're far less likely to kill you than people, and are (probably) the least of your worries…

PARASITES

Yes, as horrible as the thought is, separate life forms can live inside us. The most common parasites are worms. There are several types of worms that can happily take up residence in your body, whether they wriggle, tickle and squirm or not. Some of the most common include:

Tapeworms are a type of flatworm that can live in the human intestinal tract. They are typically contracted by eating raw or undercooked meat, especially pork, beef, or fish. A man suffering from headaches was found to have a 12cm live tapeworm in his brain and had to undergo an operation to remove it. It had been estimated to have been growing inside him for 10 years or more. A tapeworm in the brain is rare, however.

Roundworms, also known as nematodes, are a parasitic worm that can live in the human intestines. They can be contracted by ingesting contaminated soil, food, or water. They can vary in length, but can grow up to two metres long.

Pinworms are a roundworm that can live in the human intestinal tract. They are commonly found in children and are spread through contaminated food, water, or by direct contact with an infected person.

Hookworms are a type of parasitic worm that can also live in the human intestinal tract. They are usually contracted from contaminated soil.

Schistosoma is a parasitic flatworm that can live in the human body, specifically in blood vessels around the bladder and bowel. This worm is typically contracted by contact with contaminated water in tropical regions.

Strongyloides is another parasitic roundworm that can live in the intestinal tract of the human body.

The majority of these worms are contracted through poor sanitation and hygiene practices, and by consuming contaminated food or water. Some of these worms can cause serious health problems if left untreated.

A good enough reason, I think, to wash your hands often and be careful what you eat…

CREEPY CRAWLIES AND FLYING INSECTS.

Mosquitoes. One of the most serious parasites that can infect the human body is the malaria-causing Plasmodium parasite, which is transmitted through the bite of infected mosquitoes. This parasite can cause fever, chills, and flu-like symptoms, and in severe cases can lead to organ failure and death. The most lethal insect, in terms of human deaths caused, is the mosquito. Mosquitoes transmit a variety of diseases such as dengue, yellow fever, zika and many others, as well as malaria, which are responsible for hundreds of thousands of deaths worldwide each year.

Other flying insects that can cause serious harm to humans include the tsetse fly, which transmits sleeping sickness, and the black fly, which can transmit river blindness.

Bees and wasps. It is possible for someone to die from numerous bee or wasp stings. This is a condition called anaphylaxis, a severe allergic reaction that can occur when someone is stung by a bee, wasp, or hornet. Anaphylaxis can cause difficulty breathing, a drop in blood pressure, and swelling of the face and throat, which can be fatal if not treated immediately with epinephrine and other medications.

However, it is relatively rare for someone to die from bee or wasp stings alone. According to the World Health Organization, most deaths from stings occur in people who are allergic to bee venom and die from anaphylactic shock. It is estimated that the number of deaths caused by bee stings range from 50 to 150 deaths per year in the United States, and around the same number from wasp stings.

It's also important to note that most bees/wasps are not aggressive and will only sting if they feel threatened. People can avoid being stung by not approaching them or wearing protective clothing.

Snakes. The most venomous snake in the world is considered to be the Inland Taipan, also known as the 'fierce snake'. One bite from this snake is said to contain enough venom to kill 100 people. But since they live in the driest areas of central Australia, luckily people rarely encounter them. It's estimated that worldwide, snake bites cause between 81,000 and 138,000 deaths each year, with the majority of deaths occurring in rural areas of developing countries.

Spiders. The Brazilian wandering spider, also known as the banana spider, is considered to be one of the most venomous spiders in the world. Its venom contains a neurotoxin that can cause loss of muscle control and breathing problems, leading to paralysis and ultimately death.

Other highly venomous spiders include the funnel web spider, the black widow spider and the brown recluse spider. These spiders are also known to be dangerous and their bites can be fatal if not treated immediately.

All spiders have fangs. Luckily the venom is usually only strong enough to kill their prey of small insects. But some larger spiders weave strong webs that can catch small creatures like bats, birds and mice.

It's important to note that not all spider bites are fatal and that many people who are bitten survive with proper medical treatment. It's also important to keep in mind that most creatures are not aggressive and will only bite if they feel threatened. And although most people are terrified of tarantulas, their bite is very unlikely to kill you, and will probably feel like a hornet sting.

OTHER NASTYS

The blood suckers. Vampire bats are a real species of bats that feed on the blood of mammals, birds, and reptiles. They are found in Central and South America, and they use their sharp teeth to make a small incision in the skin of their prey and then lick up the blood that flows out.

Another creature that feeds on blood is the leech. Leeches are bloodsucking parasitic worms that are found in freshwater environments. They attach themselves to fish, amphibians, reptiles, birds, and mammals, and suck blood from them. Leeches are used in medicine for bloodletting and to remove blood clots.

Insects such as mosquitoes, ticks, and lice also feed on blood. They pierce the skin of their host with a specialised mouthpart called a proboscis, and suck blood through it. These insects are known to transmit several diseases such as Malaria, Yellow fever, and Lyme disease.

From the sea. The most lethal sea creature in terms of human deaths is likely to be the box jellyfish, also known as the marine stinger or sea wasp. Its venomous tentacles can cause severe pain, heart failure, and death in just a few minutes. Box jellyfish are found mostly in the coastal waters of northern Australia, Thailand and Malaysia. They are responsible for more deaths in Australia than sharks, crocodiles, and snakes combined.

Another sea creature that can cause human deaths is the Irukandji jellyfish, a small and highly venomous species found in the waters of northern Australia and the north-eastern coast of South America. Its venom can cause severe pain, heart failure, and death.

Also, the cone snail, a marine gastropod mollusk, is capable of causing human deaths with its venom, which contains a neurotoxin. The venom can cause paralysis and respiratory failure, leading to death if not treated promptly.

Sharks, probably the most feared sea creatures (the film 'Jaws' didn't help), are very unlikely to attack people unprovoked. Worldwide, there are usually less than 80 attacks a year, and often the figure is much lower. Not all attacks are fatal, either. Compare that to the number of sharks humans kill each year – around 100 million. Puts things into perspective, I think.

While some sea creatures can be dangerous to humans, most sea creatures do not pose a significant threat and attacks on humans are relatively rare. They should be much more scared of us. This leads me onto…

Mammals. Your fellow human beings are the most lethal creatures on the planet, causing millions of deaths to other humans, mammals, and creatures every year. Humans are responsible for a wide range of deaths, both directly and indirectly, through wars, murders, accidents, and other forms of violence. Additionally, human activities such as farming, deforestation, pollution, and climate change also significantly impact the number of deaths of other animals.

But if we discount humans, the most lethal mammal in terms of human deaths is likely to be the crocodile, responsible for thousands of deaths annually, mostly in Africa and Asia. These animals are known to attack humans who venture too close to their territory or who accidentally fall into the water where they live. They are known to be aggressive and powerful predators, and their bites can be fatal. Crocodiles are thought to have lived for millions of years – even alongside the dinosaurs. They can live to be around 75 years old, and the Saltwater Crocodile can grow up to 23.0 ft (7.0 m) in length.

Another mammal that can cause human deaths is the hippopotamus, responsible for around 500 deaths annually, mostly in Africa, they are known to attack boats and people who venture too close to their territory, their large size and powerful jaws make them capable of causing severe injury or death.

It's worth noting that in general, most animals do not pose a significant threat to humans, and attacks on people are relatively rare.

Monster Menagerie.
(Imagined and real...)

Monsters have been a part of human culture since the dawn of time, inspiring legends, myths, and cautionary tales for generations. Some are born from our deepest fears and anxieties, while others are based on real creatures that have roamed the earth for thousands of years. Whether they are the stuff of legend or the result of scientific fact, monsters have captured our imaginations and left an indelible mark on our collective psyche. So here we explore the fascinating world of monsters - both real and imagined - and discover stories and legends that have captivated us for centuries.

THE LOCH NESS MONSTER

Also known as Nessie, is a legendary creature said to inhabit Loch Ness in the Scottish Highlands. Those who claim to have seen Nessie typically describe her as being large and serpentine, with a long neck and one or more humps protruding from the water. Some say the Loch Ness monster is a prehistoric creature that has survived to the present day.

The legend of the Loch Ness Monster can be traced back to the 6th century AD, when Irish monk St. Columba is said to have encountered a "water beast" in the River Ness. Sightings of the creature have been reported throughout history, but the modern legend of the Loch Ness Monster began in 1933, when a road was built along the side of the loch and more sightings were reported.

Most scientists believe that they can explain the reported sightings of the creature as misidentifications of known animals, such as otters or large fish, or as hoaxes or mistaken observations.

The Loch Ness Monster is one of the most famous examples of cryptozoology, the study of animals that are not recognised by science, or thought to be extinct. While there is no scientific evidence to support the existence of the Loch Ness Monster, the legend remains a popular subject of interest and speculation.

THE SASQUATCH

Legends describe the Sasquatch, also known as Bigfoot, as inhabiting the dense forests of North America. They describe the creature as a large, ape-like creature with shaggy fur and a strong, unpleasant odour. There have been countless reported sightings of Sasquatch over the years, with some claiming to have seen it wandering through the woods, while others have reported finding large, human-like footprints.

THE YETI

A similar infamous monster is the Yeti, also known as the Abominable Snowman, which is said to inhabit the snowy mountain ranges of the Himalayas. The creature is described as a large, ape-like creature with white fur and a height of up to 10 feet.

THE CHUPACABRA

The Chupacabra is a legendary creature said to inhabit parts of the Americas, particularly in Mexico, Puerto Rico, and the United States. People describe it as a quadrupedal creature, with spines or quills running down its back, and say it has fangs and glowing red eyes. The Chupacabra is said to be a predator that feeds on the blood of livestock, particularly goats, hence its name, which means "goat sucker" in Spanish.

Said to be a mysterious creature, it has been the subject of several sightings and encounters over the years, and is described as having a fierce appearance and a powerful bite. Some people believe that it's a genetic mutation or a hybrid of different animals, while others believe it's an extra-terrestrial creature.

THE KRAKEN

Deep beneath the waves of the sea, in the murky depths where the light cannot reach, lurks a monster of unspeakable horror: the Kraken. This colossal creature, with its writhing tentacles and gaping maw, strikes fear into the hearts of sailors and sea-faring folk the world over. Legend has it that the Kraken is a giant cephalopod, a creature that resembles a monstrous octopus or squid, with eyes that glow like the light of the moon.

It lies in wait in the dark, cold waters of the ocean, biding its time until it can emerge and wreak havoc upon unsuspecting ships and their crews. It is said that the monster possesses a cunning intelligence, and that it uses its many limbs to drag ships and their passengers down into the depths, where they are devoured whole. Its tentacles can wrap around the hull of a ship, crushing it like a tin can, and its beak can tear through steel and wood as easily as flesh.

But is the Kraken real? Or is it just a fishing tale, a yarn of the sea-weary? Perhaps it's just a giant squid or large octopus, with a dose of sailors' drunken exaggeration. Only you can decide.

THE WENDIGO

The Wendigo is a supernatural creature from the folklore of the Algonquian people, said to dwell in the northern forests of North America, particularly in the Great Lakes region and the northern Midwest. It's described as a gaunt, emaciated creature, tall and thin with elongated limbs, glowing eyes, and sharp teeth. It's said to be covered in a thick layer of fur, with a long, thin nose and a tongue that hangs out of its mouth.

The Wendigo is said to be a malevolent spirit that preys on humans, particularly those who are lost in the wilderness. It can apparently drive people to madness and is said to have a powerful hunger for human flesh. It's also believed that the Wendigo can possess people and drive them to commit terrible acts, including murder and cannibalism.

It is claimed to be a powerful spirit that can control the cold and the wind, and can cause extreme cold and blizzards to strike at will. It's also said that the Wendigo can only be defeated by someone who is pure of heart and brave enough to face it. Some legends say it can only be defeated by someone who is able to outsmart it, such as by tricking it into revealing its true form.

An important figure in Algonquian folklore for centuries, it continues to capture the imagination of people today. It's featured in the famous novel "Wendigo" by Algernon Blackwood.

THE KELPIE

The Kelpie is a shape-shifting water monster from Scottish folklore that is said to reside in lochs, rivers and other bodies of water. It is often described as a horse, and it is said that it can change its appearance to lure unsuspecting travellers into the water. Once a person climbs on its back, the Kelpie drags them into the depths of the water, never to be seen again. With a powerful and hypnotic gaze that can lure even the most sceptical, the Kelpie can take many forms, including that of a handsome young man or a beautiful woman to lure travellers into its grasp.

The Kelpie has been an important figure in Scottish folklore for centuries. A famous work featuring the Kelpie is "The Kelpie's Pearls" by Mary Stewart.

FRANKENSTEIN'S MONSTER

In the dark, stormy laboratory of the mad scientist, Dr. Frankenstein, there arose a creation of monstrous proportions. With a bolt of lightning and a burst of electricity, the Frankenstein monster was born - a hideous creature of flesh and bone, pieced together from the bodies of the dead.

This terrifying figure, with its hulking form and stitched-together skin, has been a staple of horror lore for over two centuries. And yet, despite being eight foot tall with bolts through his neck, there is something oddly endearing about this lumbering behemoth, with its childlike curiosity and earnest desire to understand the world around it.

But the Frankenstein monster came from the pages of a book – the mind of Mary Shelley. So we know he isn't real – don't we?

PRE-HISTORIC MONSTERS

This chapter wouldn't be complete without mentioning some pre-historic monsters. They may not be here now, but they were definitely real in the past. Millions of years ago, long before humans, they ruled the world. Here are five of the most terrifying prehistoric monsters to ever walk the planet:

Tyrannosaurus Rex - With its massive jaws and razor-sharp teeth, the T-Rex was the ultimate predator, capable of taking down even the largest prey with ease. Standing up to 20 feet tall and weighing up to 14,000 pounds, this king of the dinosaurs was a true force to be reckoned with.

Megalodon - This ancient shark, thought to have lived around 2.6 million years ago, was the largest predator the ocean has ever seen. With teeth up to seven inches long and a body that could grow up to 60 feet in length, the Megalodon was a true terror of the deep.

Spinosaurus - With its massive sail-like back and long, crocodile-like snout, the Spinosaurus was one of the deadliest dinosaurs of all time. Able to hunt both on land and in water, this prehistoric monster was a true predator

Titanoboa - This massive snake, thought to have lived around 58 million years ago, could grow up to 40 feet in length and weigh as much as a small car. With its incredible strength and size, the Titanoboa was capable of taking down even the largest prey with ease.

Deinotherium - This prehistoric elephant, with its long, curved tusks and massive size, was one of the most intimidating creatures of its time. Standing up to 18 feet tall and weighing over 20,000 pounds, the Deinotherium was a true giant, capable of crushing anything that stood in its way.

So if you ever find yourself transported back in time to the age of the dinosaurs, beware these prehistoric monsters, for they were the true kings of the Earth. With their incredible size, strength, and ferocity, they ruled the world long before we humans were even here.

So there you have it, my friend. Have you decided which are the real, and which are the imagined? Or maybe, like me, you think they all exist... even if it *is* only in the dark and dusty corners of our imaginations...

Shall I call the Doctor?

(Illnesses, surgery, death, near-death experiences and more...)

In life, we are all bound by an inevitable fate, a force that creeps silently in the night and touches us all. It is the shadow of illness and death, the reminder that our time in this world is limited, and that one day, we must all face our final breath. This is a chapter of random facts and information about illness, disease and the end of life, about the pain and suffering that come with it, and how we try to cope. It looks at the science of death and the mysteries that still surround it, our human fears and hopes… and the fragility of our existence.

ILLNESSES AND DISEASE.

Throughout history, mankind has been subjected to the pain and distress of illness and disease. Below is a random selection of some of the worst:

Plague (Black Death): In the year 1348, a black shadow descended upon Europe, a harbinger of death and destruction. It was the Black Death, a pandemic that would sweep across the continent, leaving a trail of misery in its wake. The disease was caused by the bacterium Yersinia pestis and was transmitted from rats to humans through fleas. The symptoms were swift and merciless, with high fever, chills, and swollen lymph nodes, known as buboes, quickly appearing in the infected. The Plague swept through cities and towns, decimating entire populations. In some areas, it is estimated that up to 60% of the population perished in just a few short years. The death toll was staggering, with millions of lives lost, and the impact of the pandemic was felt for decades to come. The shortage of labour caused by the loss of life led to widespread economic disruption and social upheaval, as well as a shift in the balance of power between lords and peasants.

The medical community was unable to find a cure for the Black Plague, and attempts at treatment were largely ineffective. The most common approach was quarantine, with the infected being confined to their homes, where they would soon succumb to the disease. In some cases, entire neighbourhoods were sealed off, and the dead were left to rot in the streets. The plague doctors, who were responsible for treating the sick, wore long robes and bird-like masks to protect themselves from the disease, a symbol of the fear and desperation of the time. One of the methods used to identify infected households was the placement of a cross on the door. The crosses, typically painted in red, indicated that the house was under quarantine and that anyone entering or leaving would be at risk of contracting the disease. The practice was instituted by local authorities in an effort to contain the spread of the pandemic, as people were encouraged to stay away from infected households.

The Black Plague remains one of the most catastrophic events in human history, a reminder of the power of disease. Its impact was felt for generations, shaping the course of history and leaving a lasting imprint on the world. It is a reminder of the dangers of pandemics and the importance of continued research and preparedness, as we face new threats to global health in the modern age.

Smallpox: Smallpox was a highly contagious disease caused by the variola virus. It is estimated that smallpox killed between 300-500 million people worldwide before being eradicated by a global vaccination campaign in the 1970s. Smallpox was spread through respiratory droplets and would cause a high fever, severe body aches, and a characteristic rash. The disease would often leave survivors with permanent scars or even blindness.

Cholera: Cholera is a bacterial disease that causes severe dehydration and can be fatal within hours if left untreated. Cholera outbreaks have occurred throughout history, including several devastating pandemics in the 19th and 20th centuries. Cholera is spread through contaminated water and causes symptoms such as watery diarrhoea, vomiting, and muscle cramps.

Tuberculosis (TB): Tuberculosis is a bacterial infection that primarily affects the lungs. It was one of the leading causes of death in the 19th and early 20th centuries and continues to be a major global health threat today, with an estimated 10 million new cases each year. TB is spread through the air when an infected person coughs or sneezes. Symptoms include persistent cough, chest pain, fatigue, and weight loss.

Influenza: Influenza, also known as the flu, is a viral infection that can cause severe illness and even death, particularly in high-risk populations such as the elderly, young children, and those with weakened immune systems. One of the deadliest flu pandemics in history was the Spanish Flu, which killed an estimated 50 million people worldwide in

1918-1919. Influenza is spread through respiratory droplets and causes symptoms such as fever, cough, fatigue, and body aches. Vaccination is the most effective way to prevent the spread of the flu.

Scurvy: A disease caused by a deficiency of vitamin C, which is essential for the production of collagen, a protein that is necessary for the formation of skin, blood vessels, and other connective tissue. The symptoms of scurvy include tiredness, muscle weakness, joint and muscle pain, and the appearance of small red or blue spots on the skin. In severe cases, the disease can cause bleeding gums, anaemia, and even death. It was a major health concern for sailors during the age of exploration when voyages at sea for months or years were common. Sailors typically ate a diet that was high in salt and preserved food, but low in fresh fruits and vegetables, which are rich sources of vitamin C. As a result, many sailors developed scurvy, which was a major cause of death on long voyages. It was responsible for the deaths of thousands of sailors between the 15th and 18th centuries. It is estimated that up to two-thirds of all sailors who died at sea during this period probably died from scurvy.

It was not until the late 18th century that the connection between scurvy and a lack of vitamin C was understood, and that citrus fruits were found to be an effective treatment for the disease. The Royal Navy began to provide sailors with limes and lemons, which helped to reduce the incidence of scurvy significantly. It is thought that this is where the term 'Limey' came from for an Englishman.

Leprosy: A chronic, progressive disease caused by the bacterium Mycobacterium leprae. The disease affects the skin, nerves, and mucous membranes, and it can lead to severe disfigurement and disability if left untreated.

The symptoms of leprosy can vary depending on the infection's type and severity. Symptoms include skin lesions and nerve damage, and if left untreated, loss of fingers, toes, and limbs, eye damage, and possible blindness.

Leprosy is primarily spread through contact with the mucous membranes of the nose and mouth of an infected person, although it can also be spread through contact with the skin. The disease is treatable with antibiotics. It is estimated that around 200,000 people today are infected with leprosy, mostly in Africa and Asia.

MEDICINE, OPERATIONS AND TRANSPLANTS.

Medicine from mould. Throughout history, people have tried to find things to help fight or cure diseases. One great discovery was that of Penicillin, the first antibiotic, which has saved countless lives. It is made from a mould. Penicillin was discovered by Alexander Fleming in 1928. He discovered that a mould called Penicillium notatum was able to kill the bacteria Staphylococcus aureus. He noticed that the bacteria couldn't grow around a spore of the mould that had accidentally contaminated one of his Petri dishes. The discovery was not initially considered of great significance by the scientific community. It wasn't until the 1940s that penicillin was mass-produced and became widely used as an antibiotic to treat bacterial infections during World War II.

Operations without anaesthetic. Another amazing breakthrough in the world of treating illness and injury was the use of anaesthetic. Before its discovery, surgery was performed while the patient was fully conscious, and the only way to manage pain was through the use of physical restraint, and the use of alcohol or opium-based painkillers. Because of this, surgical procedures were often limited to those that could be completed quickly and with minimal pain to the patient. Surgery was generally only performed as a last resort, and many conditions that are now treated surgically were considered untreatable. Common surgical procedures before anaesthetics included amputations, trepanations, and the removal of bladder stones.

Anaesthetics, which are drugs or other substances used to induce a state of unconsciousness or insensitivity to pain, weren't in use until the early 19th century. The first successful use of inhaled ether as an anaesthetic was demonstrated by a dentist, William Morton in 1846. The use of anaesthetics revolutionised surgery by making it possible to perform more complex procedures that would otherwise be unbearable for patients. It also allowed for longer and more precise surgeries, which in turn led to better outcomes and fewer complications. The invention of anaesthetics was a major advancement in medicine and greatly improved the safety and efficacy of surgical procedures. Be thankful you weren't born before 1846!

Organ transplants. The first successful human organ transplant was in 1954 when a man donated his kidney to his identical twin brother. This showed that transplants were possible and led to thousands more kidney transplants and eventually the transplant of other organs, including the heart in 1967.

Today, many organs and tissues can be transplanted, including the liver, lungs, pancreas, bones, and skin. More recently, hand and full-face transplants have been completed, the first successful face transplant being performed in 2005 in France. Since then, many face transplants have been performed worldwide and the procedure has become more refined with better results. It is still considered a highly complex and risky procedure, but it has also been life-changing for many patients with severe facial disfigurement.

Will a full head transplant ever be possible? It's certainly not possible at present. The concept of a full head transplant, which would involve transplanting one person's head onto another person's body, is highly speculative and has not yet been successfully performed. The procedure would be extremely complex and would involve connecting the blood vessels, nerves, and spinal cord of the head to those of the body. The main issues with a full head transplant are the technical difficulties involved in connecting the spinal cord and the brain to the new body, as well as the ethical and psychological issues that would arise from such a procedure. The possibility of a successful head transplant is highly speculative, and there is no scientific evidence to support the idea that it can be done successfully, or ever will be.

DEATH

According to the World Health Organization, the top three leading causes of death worldwide are:

Cardiovascular diseases, including heart disease and stroke, account for more than 17.9 million deaths per year. These diseases are caused by a variety of factors, including unhealthy diet, lack of physical activity, tobacco use, and high blood pressure.

Cancer is the second leading cause of death worldwide, accounting for 9.6 million deaths per year. Cancer is caused by changes (mutations) to the genes of DNA inside a person. The majority of cancers cannot be prevented, but some things may predispose you to cancer, such as exposure to certain chemicals and substances, or unhealthy lifestyle choices such as tobacco use, a bad diet, and lack of physical activity.

Respiratory diseases, such as chronic obstructive pulmonary disease (COPD) and pneumonia, account for 3.9 million deaths per year. These diseases can sometimes be caused by exposure to air pollution, smoking, or by respiratory infection.

These figures are estimates and may vary. It's also important to note that many of these deaths are preventable through early detection, prevention and control of risk factors, and access to proper health care.

The most common causes of death by unnatural causes are accidents, (including car accidents, falls, and drowning), suicide, and murder/manslaughter.

QUESTIONS WE ASK…

Can someone die of fright? Someone can die from fear, or more accurately from the effects of fear, although it is relatively rare. Fear can cause several physical and emotional reactions, such as increased heart rate, high blood pressure, and anxiety, which can lead to a condition known as "sudden death" or "death from fright".

Sudden death from fright can occur when the body's stress response is triggered, releasing a flood of stress hormones such as adrenaline and cortisol. These hormones can cause a rapid increase in heart rate and blood pressure, which can lead to heart attack or stroke, especially in people with underlying health conditions such as heart disease.

Can someone appear dead when they're not?

Several medical conditions and drugs can cause a person to appear as if they are dead. Some of these include:

Catatonia: A state of abnormal motor behaviour characterized by stupor or rigidity, it can be caused by certain medical conditions such as schizophrenia, bipolar disorder, severe depression, or by certain medications. Individuals in a catatonic state may appear unresponsive, immobile, or even dead.

Coma: A state of unconsciousness from which a person cannot be awakened. Coma can be caused by brain injury, infection, metabolic disorders, or other medical conditions.

Drug overdose: Certain drugs, such as opioids and sedatives, can cause a person to appear as if they are dead if they are taken in large enough quantities.

Hyperkalemia: This is a condition where the potassium level in the blood is too high, which can cause cardiac arrest and make a person appear dead.

Has anyone been buried alive? It is probable that the possibility of being alive whilst appearing dead led to people's fear of being buried alive. These days, we have sophisticated methods to ensure the correct diagnosis of death, but this wasn't the case in the past.

The fear of being buried alive, also known as taphophobia, is a deep-seated fear that has gripped the human psyche for centuries. The thought of being entombed alive in a dark, cold grave is nothing short of terrifying. The idea of being trapped in a cramped, suffocating space, with no way to escape or call for help, is a horror that haunts many of us.

Throughout history, people have gone to great lengths to ensure they weren't buried alive. From safety coffins to grave alarms, people have devised all sorts of contraptions to ensure they'd be able to signal for help if they were mistakenly buried alive.

There have been several historical accounts of people being buried alive, either by mistake or as a result of being falsely pronounced dead. This was a common fear, particularly in the 18th and 19th centuries, when the medical understanding of death was not as advanced as it is today.

In the past, people were sometimes buried prematurely, because the signs of death were not clearly understood and there were no reliable methods of determining death. This was especially true in cases of drowning, suffocation, or hanging, where the individual may have appeared dead but was still alive.

Additionally, some cultures have had the practice of "live burials" as a form of punishment or execution. Some have been buried alive as a punishment for crimes such as treason, rebellion, or witchcraft.

Today, the determination of death is based on strict criteria, such as the absence of a heartbeat, breathing, and brain activity, and the use of modern technology, such as an electrocardiogram (ECG) and brain-stem death testing, has made it much less likely for someone to be buried alive by mistake. However, it did happen as recently as 2014. A 49-year-old woman was buried alive after being declared dead due to cancer. Shortly after her burial, her family reported hearing her scream from under the earth at the cemetery. An investigation found that she died of heart failure inside her coffin. The medication given to her as part of her cancer treatment caused her to be declared clinically dead by mistake.

How long does a human body take to decompose? The rate of decomposition of a human body can vary greatly depending on several factors, such as the environment, weather conditions, and the presence of insects or animals.

In general, a human body begins to decompose soon after death, with the initial stages of decomposition happening rapidly. Within minutes, the body will start to cool as blood flow stops and the body's metabolic processes come to a halt.

In the first hours after death, the body will begin to change colour as blood pools in the lower parts of the body. Rigor mortis, the stiffening of the muscles, sets in within 2-6 hours after death, and usually lasts for 24-48 hours.

After the first 24 hours, the body starts to release gases, which can cause the body to bloat and take on a greenish or purplish colour.

If the body is exposed to the elements and not refrigerated, the process of decomposition accelerates. After a few days, the body starts to release fluids and the skin and soft tissues start to break down, creating a strong, unpleasant odour. The body will become a host for insects and other scavengers, including flies, maggots, and beetles, which will further accelerate the decomposition process.

If the body is buried underground or in a sealed casket, the decomposition process is slowed down, but it will still occur. Depending on the conditions of the soil, the casket, and whether there is embalming, a buried body can take several decades to fully decompose.

What is Embalming? The oldest known embalmed body ever found is that of a female priestess who lived in the Han dynasty (206 BC - 220 AD) in ancient China. Her body was discovered in 1971 in a tomb sealed for roughly 2,000 years. The body was extremely well-preserved. The embalming included removing the internal organs, treating the body with a mixture of herbs, and wrapping it in layers of linen. The preservation technique was so effective that her hair, nails, and skin were still intact, and her facial features were still recognisable.

Sometimes, bodies are still embalmed today. It's a process in which a deceased person's body is preserved through the injection of chemicals and other treatments. It is typically done to delay the decomposition of the body and make it suitable for viewing during a funeral or wake. Embalming is also done when a death is considered suspicious, or when the body will be transported over a long distance. The process of embalming involves the injection of embalming fluid, which typically consists of a mixture of formaldehyde, water, and other chemicals, into the

deceased's bloodstream. This fluid helps to preserve
the body by slowing down the decomposition process
and by killing any bacteria that may be present.

NEAR-DEATH EXPERIENCES.

Many people hope for or believe in an 'afterlife' – that
death is not the end. Most religions support this
belief, and some people claim to have had near-death
experiences that indicate an afterlife exists. But did
they really? Or was it just imaginings… or a dream?
Or as some claim, the effects of lack of oxygen,
drugs, or anaesthetic? Perhaps we will never know…
but some accounts are very convincing.

The idea of death has always been shrouded
in mystery and fear, but what happens when we come
close to death and are then granted a reprieve? Near-
death experiences, also known as NDEs, have been
reported by millions of people around the world, each
with a unique tale to tell.

For some, NDEs are vivid, life-changing
experiences that bring newfound perspective and
spiritual awareness. For others, they are confusing,
disorienting encounters with an unknown realm. But
regardless of their nature, NDEs have been
documented and studied by medical professionals,
philosophers, and theologians alike.

Here are three real-life examples of near-
death experiences that demonstrate the incredible
range of emotions, sensations, and memories
associated with NDEs.

Sarah, aged 32, was in a terrible car accident
that left her unconscious and on the brink of death.
As she floated in a deep, dark void, she suddenly saw
a warm light that beckoned her closer. As she

approached the light, she felt a sense of comfort and peace like she had never known before. She felt as though the light was calling to her, drawing her towards it. Sarah eventually returned to consciousness and was shocked to discover that her heart had stopped for a short time.

Tom was a soldier who had survived multiple tours in combat zones. But it was a routine medical procedure that nearly took his life. As he floated above his body, he watched the medical team rush to save him, the beeps of the machine monitoring his heart growing slower and slower. Suddenly, he was transported to a beautiful, peaceful garden, where he met his deceased mother. They hugged and talked, and she reassured him that everything was going to be alright. He felt a sense of overwhelming love and peace, before suddenly waking up back in his body, the medical team successfully reviving him.

Jane was in her 20s when she was diagnosed with a serious illness that left her with only a few months to live. In her darkest moments, she felt herself slipping away, and as she did, she entered a dark tunnel. At first, she was afraid, but as she travelled deeper into the tunnel, she saw a light at the end, growing brighter. Suddenly, she felt herself being pulled towards the light, and as she emerged, she was surrounded by a feeling of love and peace she had never known before. She eventually recovered from her illness, and attributes her survival to the powerful experience she had in the tunnel.

These examples of near-death experiences show just a fraction of the range of experiences people have reported. Whether they are seen as spiritual encounters or simply a result of brain function, NDEs continue to captivate and intrigue us all. And as we continue to explore this mysterious and often frightening realm, we may yet uncover the secrets of what happens when we brush with death… and what lies beyond.

Is there any justice?

(Wrongful execution, prisons, the persecution of witches...)

This is a serious chapter as the subject matter involves truly heinous acts. Hopefully, if humanity continues to remember and condemn these terrible miscarriages of justice and acts of torture and persecution, it will reduce the likelihood of such horrendous things happening in the future.

WRONGFUL EXECUTION.

There have been many wrongful executions around the world.

One of the most horrendous cases in British history helped lead to the abolition of the death sentence in Britain. Timothy John Evans was a Welshman who was wrongly accused of murdering his wife and infant daughter at their home in London. In January 1950, Evans was tried and convicted of the murder of his daughter and was executed by hanging on 9 March 1950. During his trial, Evans accused his downstairs neighbour, John Christie, who was the chief prosecution witness, of committing the murders. Three years later, Christie was found to be a serial killer. He had murdered several other women in the same house, including his own wife. Christie was himself sentenced to death, and while awaiting execution, he confessed to murdering Mrs Evans. An official inquiry concluded in 1966 that Christie had probably murdered Evans's daughter, Geraldine, and Evans was granted a posthumous pardon.

The case generated much controversy and was acknowledged to be a terrible miscarriage of justice. Along with the cases of Derek Bentley and Ruth Ellis, the case played a major part in the removal of capital punishment for murder in Britain in 1965.

This case and other crimes of the serial killer John Christie, were dramatised in the chilling film 10 Rillington Place, made in 1971 and starring Richard Attenborough, Judy Geeson, and John Hurt.

Another terrible case of wrongful execution was that of Jesse Tafero in America, who was convicted of murder and executed by electric chair in May 1990 in Florida for the murders of a highway Patrol officer and a Canadian constable. The conviction of a co-defendant was overturned in 1992 after a recreation of the crime scene indicated a third person had committed the murders. Not only was Tafero wrongly accused, his electric chair malfunctioned, causing his head to catch on fire. After this, a debate was focused around humane methods of execution and lethal injections became more common in the states rather than the electric chair.

In China, Wei Qing'an, a 23-year-old Chinese citizen was executed for the rape of Kun Liu, a woman who had disappeared. The execution was carried out on 3 May 1984. In the next month, Tian Yuxiu was arrested and admitted that he had committed the rape. Three years later, Wei was officially declared innocent.

These are just a few examples of wrongful executions that have occurred worldwide.

WRONGFUL IMPRISONMENT.

In America, according to the Death Penalty Information Centre, there have been over 150 people who were sentenced to death and later exonerated in the US since 1973. Some of these people were released after serving many years in prison, while others were released just days before their scheduled execution.

Similarly, in other countries, people have been sentenced to death and later found to be innocent. In some cases, this is due to new evidence coming to light, such as DNA testing, which can prove a person's innocence. In other cases, it is due to misconduct or errors in the legal system.

There have been many incidences of wrongful imprisonment. One case of note in America was that of Darryl Hunt. He was convicted of the murder of Deborah Sykes in 1984. Hunt's girlfriend initially provided an alibi for him, but later said Hunt had told her he had killed Sykes. She recanted this false statement before Hunt's trial, but he was still convicted.

In 1994, DNA testing showed that Hunt's DNA did not match that of the killer, but his appeals were rejected. It wasn't until 2004 that the killer's DNA profile was matched to another convicted murderer, who later admitted he had murdered Deborah Sykes. Darryl Hunt was finally released from prison in 2005 having served 20 years for a crime he did not commit.

In Canada, a well-known wrongful conviction is the case of David Milgaard, who, at the age of 16, was convicted of murdering Gail Miller. He spent 23 years in prison and waited an extra 5 years for the DNA evidence that proved his innocence in 1997. Two years later, Larry Fisher who lived in the area was found guilty of murdering Gail Miller.

THE SMALLEST PRISON.

One of the most extreme examples of small prison cells is the 'standing cell' or 'oubliette' (French for 'to forget') used during the medieval period. These cells were often no more than a small, narrow room that was just big enough for a person to stand in. Sometimes they were so narrow that the prisoner couldn't even turn around. Often, they would just be a hole in the ground with a trapdoor at the top which was out of reach of the prisoner. Prisoners were sometimes kept in these cells for long periods of time, and 'forgotten about'. They could be subjected to extreme temperatures and lack of light, sanitation, and food. These type of prison cells have also been used in more modern times, for example in World War Two in the Nazi concentration camp of Auschwitz. There are examples of medieval standing cells in Warwick Castle, England and in Bastille, France.

Today, the use of small and inhumane prison conditions are prohibited by international human rights laws, and are considered as a form of torture.

THE LONGEST SERVING PRISONER.

It is difficult to accurately determine who has been in prison the longest due to incomplete records from the past. However, Charles Foussard (born in 1882) was a

French Australian man, who spent most of his life confined in a mental asylum in Victoria, Australia, after murdering an elderly man and stealing his boots. He died while still incarcerated at 92 years of age, making this the longest recorded continuous served prison sentence in the world.

Foussard was born in New Caledonia around 1882, and worked on ships as a young man. In 1899, he deserted his ship the St. Elizabeth while it was docked in Sydney, and spent the next few years as a vagrant, supporting himself by occasional labouring work and petty theft.

On 28 June 1903, he murdered an elderly man shooting him with a pea-rifle, and then stealing his boots. He was found by police and Aboriginal trackers in possession of the distinctive boots, and charged with the elderly man's murder.

Under interrogation, Foussard claimed that he had also murdered an Indian hawker. He later withdrew parts of this claim, but when taken to the site of the murder demonstrated a good knowledge of the location, including aspects which had changed since the incident. At his committal hearing, the government medical officer stated that Foussard was of unsound mind and prone to delusions, and was thus unfit to stand trial. He was committed to the J Ward prison for the criminally insane in Ararat, where he remained for the rest of his life. At his death in 1974, he had spent over 70 years in custody.

METHODS OF EXECUTION.

Over thousands of years, humans have devised many methods of killing other human beings. Thankfully, most of these methods are now illegal and no longer practiced. Some methods from history include:

Burnt at the stake is a method of execution in which a person is tied to a large wooden stake and then set on fire. Historically, this method was used to punish those accused of witchcraft, heresy, and other crimes. The burning would be slow and painful, often taking several hours for the person to die.

Hung, drawn and quartered was a method of execution that was used in medieval England, typically for treason. The person would be hanged by the neck until almost dead, then disembowelled and their entrails burned in front of them, before being beheaded and quartered (cut into four pieces).

The guillotine is a method of execution that involves the use of a large mechanical device with a sharp blade that drops to sever the head from the body. This method was used in France from the late 18th century to the late 20th century, the last execution by guillotine in France was in 1977.

Decapitation by sword or axe is a method of execution in which a person's head is severed from their body using a sharp blade. This method has been used throughout history, and is still used in some countries today.

Lethal injection is a method of execution in which a person is injected with a combination of drugs that cause death. This method is considered more humane than others, and is currently used in several US states and other countries.

The electric chair is a method of execution in which a person is strapped to a chair and then subjected to a high-voltage electrical current. This method was used in the United States as a more humane alternative to hanging, but has been largely discontinued in favour of lethal injection as the primary method of execution.

Poison is a method of execution in which a person is given a toxic substance, usually by ingestion, which causes death. This method has been used throughout history for both legal and illegal killings.

Hanging is a method of execution in which a person is suspended by the neck from a rope or noose until death. This method has been used throughout history and is still used in some countries today.

A firing squad is a method of execution in which a group of individuals shoot a person with firearms, typically at close range. This method is still used in some countries for military and capital punishment.

Strangulation is a method of execution in which a person's air supply is cut off by means of a cord, rope or other device, causing death by asphyxiation. This method has been used throughout history and is still used in some countries today, typically in conjunction with hanging.

Asphyxiation is a method of execution in which a person's air supply is cut off, causing death by suffocation. This method can be done through various means, like hanging, suffocation with a plastic bag or by gassing.

Bomb is a method of execution in which a person is killed by an explosive device. This method is typically used in acts of terrorism or warfare, and is illegal in most countries.

THE PERSECUTION OF 'WITCHES'.

Witchcraft wasn't made a capital offence in Britain until 1563, although it was deemed heresy and was denounced as such by Pope Innocent VIII in 1484. From 1484 until around 1750 some 200,000 witches were tortured, burnt or hanged in Western Europe.

Most supposed witches were usually old women, and invariably poor. Any who were unfortunate enough to be 'crone-like' were assumed to possess the 'Evil Eye'. If they also had a cat this was taken a proof, as witches always had a 'familiar', the cat being the most common.

Many unfortunate women were condemned on this sort of evidence and hanged after undergoing appalling torture. The 'pilnie-winks' (thumb screws) and iron 'caspie-claws' (a form of leg irons heated over a brazier) usually got a 'confession' from the supposed witch.

Witch fever gripped East Anglia for 14 terrible months between 1645 – 1646. The people of these eastern counties were solidly Puritan and rabid anti-Catholics and easily swayed by bigoted preachers whose mission was to seek out the slightest whiff of heresy. A man called Matthew Hopkins, an unsuccessful lawyer, became known as the 'Witchfinder General'. He had 68 people put to death in Bury St. Edmunds alone, and 19 hanged at Chelmsford in a single day. After Chelmsford, he set off for Norfolk and Suffolk. Aldeburgh paid him £6 for clearing the town of witches, Kings Lynn £15 and a grateful Stowmarket £23. This was at a time when the daily wage was 2.5p.

A heart carved on a wall in the marketplace at Kings Lynn is supposed to mark the spot where the heart of Margaret Read, a condemned witch who was being burnt at the stake, leaped from the flames and struck the wall.

Much of Matthew Hopkins's theories of deduction were based on Devil's Marks. A wart or mole or even a flea bite he took to be a Devil's Mark and used his 'jabbing needle' to see if these marks were insensitive to pain. His 'needle' was a 3-inch-long spike that retracted into the spring-loaded handle so the unfortunate woman never felt any pain.

There were other unfair tests for witches. Mary Sutton of Bedford was put to the swimming test. With her thumbs tied to opposite big toes she was flung into the river. If she floated she was guilty, if she sank, innocent. Poor Mary floated.

A last reminder of Hopkins' reign of terror was discovered in St. Osyth, Essex, in 1921. Two female skeletons were found in a garden, pinned into unmarked graves and with iron rivets driven through their joints. This was to make sure a witch could not return from the grave. Hopkins was responsible for over 300 executions.

Mother Shipton is remembered still in Knaresborough, Yorkshire. Although called a witch, she is more famous for her predictions about the future. She apparently foresaw cars, trains, planes and the telegraph. Her cave and the Dripping Well, where objects hung under the dripping water become like stone, are a popular site to visit today in Knaresborough.

In August 1612, the Pendle Witches, three generations of one family, were marched through the crowded streets of Lancaster and hanged.

Witch trials also occurred in the English colonies, where English law was applied. This was particularly the case in The Thirteen Colonies in North America. Examples of these were the Connecticut Witch Trials from 1647 to 1663. The most famous of these trials were the Salem witch trials in 1692.

Though many of the Acts against witchcraft were repealed in 1736, witch hunting still went on. In 1863, an alleged male witch was drowned in a pond in Headingham, Essex and in 1945 the body of an elderly farm labourer was found near the village of Meon Hill in Warwickshire. His throat had been cut and his corpse was pinned to the earth with a pitchfork. The murder remains unsolved, however the man was reputed, locally, to be a wizard.

It's important to note that the term 'witch' is used in different ways and can have different meanings depending on the context, and the portrayal of witches in popular culture often differs from their historical and cultural background. The idea of witches as evil, supernatural beings who use their powers for harm, is a stereotype that has been used to try to justify persecution and violence.

Many Wiccans, a contemporary pagan new religious movement, consider themselves witches and identify with the tradition of witchcraft.

In most countries, witchcraft is no longer considered a crime and there is no legal punishment for practicing it, so I'm off to trade in my car for a broomstick…

Unsolved murders.

(A few of the many).

It must be truly horrendous for a member of your family, or a friend, to be murdered. Perhaps it is even worse when the murderer is never identified, for it doesn't allow any form of 'closure' for the family, nor is justice served if the murderer is never tried. Sadly, there are many unsolved murders. A random selection of cases follows.

The Hinterkaifeck murders.
Hinterkaifeck farm, located in a remote area of Germany, was owned by Andreas Gruber, a well-respected farmer. On the evening of March 31, 1922, Andreas, his wife Cazilia, their daughter Viktoria, and Viktoria's two children, Cazilia and Josef, were brutally murdered on the farm.

    The bodies were discovered several days later, after neighbours noticed that no one had been seen coming or going from the farm. When authorities arrived at the scene, they found the bodies in the barn, brutally beaten and covered in hay.

    What made the murders even more chilling was the fact that the family had heard strange noises and seen footprints in the snow leading up to the house in the days leading up to the crime. Andreas had even found a newspaper on the property that he couldn't account for.

    The brutal nature of the murders at Hinterkaifeck shocked the nation and sparked a massive investigation that lasted for years. However, despite the efforts of the police, the killer was never found.

Some aspects of the crime scene suggested that the killer may have stayed on the farm for several days after the murders. Neighbours reported seeing smoke coming from the chimney of the farmhouse in the days after the murders, and the animals on the farm were still being fed.

Police interviewed over 100 suspects in the years following the murders, but none were charged. One of the most promising leads came in the form of a letter sent to the police in 1923, claiming responsibility for the murders. The letter was written in a peculiar mix of German and Bavarian dialect, and the author claimed to be a soldier who had returned from the First World War with a grudge against Andreas Gruber. However, the letter did not provide any concrete evidence, and its author was never identified.

In 2007, a team of German police officers reopened the case and conducted a thorough search of the farm. They used modern forensic techniques to analyse evidence from the crime scene, including hairs found on the victims' bodies. However, the investigation once again failed to turn up any new leads, and the case remains unsolved.

The murders have since become a notorious true crime case in Germany and the subject of numerous books and documentaries.

The Hinterkaifeck farm was eventually torn down, and a memorial now stands in its place.

The Isdal woman.

On November 29, 1970, a man and his two daughters were hiking in the Isdalen Valley near Bergen,

Norway when they stumbled upon the burned body of a woman. The woman's death was immediately deemed suspicious, as her clothes had been partially burnt and there were indications that she had been poisoned. Additionally, the woman had no identification on her person, and the labels on her clothes had been removed.

Despite extensive efforts by Norwegian authorities, the identity of the Isdal Woman remains a mystery to this day. The investigation was complicated by the fact that the woman had used several false identities during her travels in Norway, including the names Claudia Tielt, Vera Schlosseneck, and Finella Lorck. She also spoke several languages fluently, leading investigators to believe that she may have been a spy.

The woman had checked into a hotel in Bergen on November 23, 1970, using the name "Fenella Lorck." She was described as being between the ages of 30 and 40, with long, dark hair and a distinctively-shaped jaw. Over the next few days, she was seen around Bergen by several witnesses, including a photographer who took a picture of her.

Investigators were able to determine that the Isdal Woman had travelled extensively throughout Europe prior to arriving in Norway. She had stayed in several hotels under false names, and had used several false passports to cross international borders. Some witnesses reported that she was often seen with several different men, leading investigators to speculate that she may have been involved in espionage.

Despite numerous leads and investigations, the identity of the Isdal Woman remains unknown. The case has become one of Norway's greatest mysteries, and has sparked countless theories and rumours about the woman's true identity and the circumstances surrounding her death.

The Villisca Axe Murders

On June 10, 1912, the Moore family and two young guests were bludgeoned to death with an axe in their home in Villisca, Iowa. The victims included Josiah and Sarah Moore, their four children, and the two young guests who were spending the night. All of the victims were found in their beds and had been struck repeatedly with the sharp end of the axe.

The murders immediately sparked a massive investigation and a nationwide manhunt for the killer. However, despite several suspects being identified, no one was ever convicted for the crime. The murders remain unsolved and have become one of the most notorious true crime cases in American history.

The killer is believed to have remained in the house for several hours after the murders, possibly even sleeping in one of the victims' beds. Additionally, it is believed that the killer may have been familiar with the Moore family and their home, as there were no signs of forced entry and the killer seemed to know the layout of the house.

In the years since the murders, several theories have been proposed about the killer's identity, including a traveling preacher named Rev. George Kelly, a serial killer named Henry Lee Moore who was active in the area at the time, and a local businessman named Frank F. Jones who was in a feud with Josiah Moore. However, none of these theories have ever been proven.

The murders were discovered by the Moore family's neighbour, Mary Peckham. She became concerned when she noticed that the Moore family's house was unusually quiet and their curtains were still drawn long after they would normally be up and about. When she tried to enter the house, she found that the doors were locked from the inside.

After the murders, the town of Villisca was thrown into a panic. Many residents began sleeping with weapons or moving out of town altogether. The town's schools were closed for several days, and several businesses closed permanently due to the negative association with the murders.

The murders have inspired several works of fiction, including the book "The Man from the Train" by Bill James and Rachel McCarthy James. In this book, the authors propose that the Villisca Axe Murders were actually part of a larger series of axe murders that took place across the United States in the early 20th century.

The Moore family's house still stands in Villisca and is now a museum dedicated to the memory of the victims. The house has been restored to its 1912 appearance, and visitors can tour the house and learn more about the murders and the investigation. The house is also said to be haunted, and has been the subject of several paranormal investigations.

The disappearance of Suzy Lamplugh.

This is one of the most high-profile unsolved cases in England. Suzy Lamplugh was a 25-year-old estate agent who disappeared on July 28, 1986, after going to meet a client at a property in Fulham, London. She was declared legally dead in 1994, but her body has never been found.

At the time of her disappearance, Suzy Lamplugh was working for Sturgis Estate Agents in London. On the day of her disappearance, she left the office to meet a client who had requested a viewing of a property on Shorrolds Road in Fulham. Suzy left her office at around 12:30 pm and was never seen again.

Two witnesses reported seeing Suzy arguing with a man outside the property on Shorrolds Road shortly before she disappeared. The man was described as being around 6 feet tall, with dark hair and aged between 35 and 40. Despite an extensive police investigation, the man was never identified.

Over the years, several suspects have been named in connection with Suzy's disappearance, but no one has ever been charged or convicted. One of the most prominent suspects was John Cannan, a convicted murderer who was released from prison on the day of Suzy Lamplugh's disappearance. Cannan was arrested in 1989 and questioned, but he was never charged due to a lack of evidence.

In 1994, the Suzy Lamplugh Trust was established by Lamplugh's parents, Paul and Diana, in her memory. The trust aims to raise awareness of personal safety and provides support to victims of stalking and harassment.

Despite numerous appeals for information and several reviews of the case over the years, the disappearance of Suzy Lamplugh remains unsolved.

The Hammersmith murders.

The Hammersmith murders were a series of six unsolved murders that took place in and around the Hammersmith area of London between 1964 and 1965. The first victim, 30-year-old Hannah Tailford, was found strangled in her bed-sit on January 2, 1964. Just over a month later, on February 8, 35-year-old Irene Lockwood was also found strangled in her bed-sit, which was located less than half a mile from Tailford's. Both women had been sexually assaulted and were found partially undressed.

On April 24, the body of Helen Barthelemy was found on the shore of the River Thames near Chiswick Bridge. She had been strangled and was also partially undressed.

On June 8, the body of Mary Fleming was found on the shore of the River Thames at Barnes. She had been strangled and was also partially undressed.

On November 23, 1964, the body of Frances Brown, 21, was found in an alleyway off King Street in Hammersmith. She had been strangled and was also partially undressed.

The final victim, Bridget O'Hara, 28, was found on February 16, 1965, in an alleyway off Fulham Palace Road. She had been strangled and was also partially undressed.

All of the victims were young women who had been strangled and sexually assaulted. The police believed that the murders were the work of a single serial killer who was targeting prostitutes.

The Hammersmith murders were a shocking and brutal series of crimes that terrorized the people of London in the early 1960s. The murders were dubbed the "Hammersmith nude murders" by the press, as several of the victims had been found partially undressed.

The police investigation into the murders was extensive, with over 3,000 people interviewed and over 7,000 statements taken. The police even launched a massive manhunt, with officers stopping and questioning over 80,000 men who matched the killer's description.

Despite their efforts, the police were unable to catch the killer. Several suspects were identified and questioned, but no one was ever charged with the murders. One of the most promising leads was a man who had been seen in the area at the time of one of the murders. He was described as being around 5'8" tall, with light brown hair, and wearing a distinctive green jacket. However, despite an extensive search, the man was never identified.

Another suspect was a local builder who had a history of violence towards women. He was questioned by police and admitted to being in the area at the time of one of the murders, but he was ultimately ruled out as a suspect due to a lack of evidence.

The Hammersmith murders were one of the first cases in which forensic science was used extensively. The police used forensic evidence to link some of the murders, but the technology available at the time was limited. The killer's DNA was never found, and advances in DNA testing in recent years have not led to any breakthroughs in the case.

The unsolved murder of Betty Shanks.

The murder case of Betty Shanks has remained a mystery in Australia for over 70 years. On September 19, 1952, Betty Shanks, a 22-year-old nurse, was walking home from work in the Brisbane suburb of Wilston when she was attacked and killed.

The circumstances of Betty Shanks' murder were particularly brutal. She was found with her throat slashed, her clothes torn, and her body left in a park close to her home. Despite an extensive investigation at the time, the case has remained unsolved, and the identity of Betty Shanks' killer remains unknown.

The investigation into Betty Shanks' murder was one of the largest in Queensland's history. The police interviewed hundreds of people, conducted door-to-door searches, and even set up roadblocks in the hope of finding a clue that would lead to the killer's identity.

Over the years, numerous theories and suspects have been put forward in relation to Betty Shanks' murder. Some have suggested that the killer may have been a local resident or someone she knew, while others believe that the murder may have been committed by a stranger passing through the area.

Despite the lack of progress in solving the case, the memory of Betty Shanks has not been forgotten. Her murder has continued to capture the attention of the public, with various media reports and documentaries exploring the case and attempting to shed new light on the events of that fateful night. Despite the passage of time, the hope remains that one day, someone will come forward with information that will finally bring closure to this tragic case.

Betty Shanks was a well-liked and respected member of the community, known for her dedication to her work as a nurse. She had just finished her shift at the Royal Brisbane Hospital and was walking home when she was attacked and murdered.

A key piece of evidence in the case was a blood-stained dress found in a nearby drain. The dress was believed to belong to Betty Shanks, but DNA testing was not available at the time to confirm this. The dress was also missing a button, and a button was found near Betty's body.

In 2002, the Queensland Police Service announced that they were reopening the investigation into the murder. They hoped that advances in forensic technology would help to shed new light on the case. However, no new leads or evidence were uncovered, and the case remains unsolved.

We can only hope that the murderers receive appropriate retribution – in this world or the next.

Mass murderers, serial killers, and gangsters.

In the shadows of society, where the streets are dark and the silence is deafening, there walk among us those who prey upon the innocent. They are cold-blooded killers who leave death and destruction in their wake. They are the mass murderers and the serial killers, the names that are whispered in hushed tones and forever buried in our minds. They are the twisted people who give in to their basest desires and bring pain and suffering to countless lives; they are the most notorious killers of our time.

The true horror of mass murderers and serial killers lies in the fact that they are not monsters from another world, but rather everyday people who live among us. They may be our neighbours, colleagues, or even our friends – who hide in plain sight.

A serial killer is defined as someone who has killed three or more people over a period of time, often in different places, with 'cooling off' periods in between. The murders are separate events, probably driven by psychological thrill or pleasure. Serial killers are often psychopaths.

Mass murderers kill many people, but typically at the same time in a single location. With some exceptions, many mass murders end with the death of the perpetrators, either by self-infliction or by police shooting. Mass murderers are generally dissatisfied people or misfits, with poor social skills and few friends. They may have personality disorders or psychopathic tendencies. Their motives are usually less obvious than those of serial killers.

Serial killers and mass murderers often display the same sort of characteristics such as manipulation and lack of empathy… as do gangsters.

Gangsters are defined as violent criminals, usually part of an organised gang that may practice extortion, blackmail, drug dealing, or other crimes for money. They are not necessarily murderers, although many commit murder or threaten it. A well-known 'gangster' organisation is the Mafia.

MASS MURDERERS.

Ask people who they think is the biggest mass murderer in history, and most will suggest Adolph Hitler or Joseph Stalin. But Chinese Mao Zedong's, 'Great Leap Forward' policy led to the deaths of up to 45 million people from 1958 to 1962, probably making it the biggest case of mass murder ever recorded. Mass murderers on a vast scale such as Hitler, Stalin, and Zedong, and the atrocities committed in their name or because of their policies, should be studied separately as they are beyond the remit of this book.

Most mass murders by an individual are by shooting. There are 15 or more mass shootings in the USA each year. There are generally more in the US than in other countries due to the availability of guns for purchase. Three infamous mass shootings are listed below:

In October 2017, in Las Vegas, America, Stephen Paddock opened fire on a crowd from his 32nd-floor room at the Mandalay Bay Resort. The rampage lasted more than 15 minutes as panicked concertgoers tried to take cover, not knowing where the shots were coming from. In all, 58 people were killed, and hundreds more were injured. When police broke into the 64-year-old gunman's room, they found he had killed himself.

In April 2007, Seung-Hui Cho killed 32 people in the Virginia Tech shooting in the United States. He was a student in Blacksburg, Virginia, and a US resident originally from South Korea. 17 other people were wounded and 6 were injured trying to escape. As the police came, Cho killed himself with a shot in the head. Cho had been declared mentally ill prior to the shootings but was still able to buy guns.

In August 1987, Michael Ryan, 27, shot and killed sixteen people, including a police officer and his own mother, in Hungerford, England. He shot fifteen more people who survived. The shootings occurred at several different locations, one of which was his old school. He finally shot himself before he could be arrested. No clear motive for his actions has ever been found.

SERIAL KILLERS.

Some infamous serial killers are listed below:

Ted Bundy was an American who murdered at least 30 young women and girls in the 1970s. He would lure his victims by pretending to be injured or disabled, and then bludgeon them with a blunt object, usually a crowbar. He was eventually captured, tried, and sentenced to death. He was executed in 1989.

John Gacy was an American who murdered at least 33 young men and boys in the 1970s. He would pretend to be a successful businessman, take them to his home and strangle them. He buried many of the bodies in the underneath space of his own home. He was arrested, tried, and sentenced to death. He was executed in 1994.

Jeffrey Dahmer was an American serial killer who murdered at least 17 young men and boys in the 1980s and 1990s. He would promise his victims money or drugs, then strangle them. He also engaged in acts of necrophilia, dismemberment, and cannibalism. He was arrested, tried and convicted, and sentenced to life imprisonment. He was killed by a fellow inmate in 1994.

Gary Ridgway, known as the "Green River Killer", was an American serial killer who murdered at least 49 women in the 1980s and 1990s. He would offer victims work or money, and then strangle them. He was arrested, tried, and sentenced to life in prison. He is now aged 74 and still serving his sentence.

Andrei Chikatilo was a Soviet serial killer who murdered at least 52 women and children in the 1980s. He would pretend to be a kindly grandfather, and then stab and mutilate his victims. He was tried, sentenced to death, and executed in 1994.

Dr Harold Shipman was a British serial killer who murdered at least 215 of his patients in the 1970s and 1980s. He would administer lethal doses of diamorphine to his victims, many of whom were elderly and in poor health. He was tried and convicted of murdering a 'sample' of 15 people, and sentenced to life in prison. He was found dead in his cell in 2004, an apparent suicide.

Jack the Ripper is the pseudonym of an unidentified serial killer who murdered at least five women, all prostitutes, in the Whitechapel district of London, England in 1888. The murders were characterised by the surgical skill used in the killings, especially in the removal of internal organs, and the fact that several of the victims were mutilated. The identity of the killer was never conclusively proven and the case remains officially unsolved.

Fred West and Rose West were a British couple who were convicted of a series of murders in the 1990s. They were responsible for the deaths of at least 12 young women and girls, many of whom were tortured and raped. The victims were mainly young women and girls, including their own daughter. They were lured to the Wests' home with promises of work or accommodation. The remains of nine victims were found buried in the garden and in the basement of the couple's home in Cromwell Street, Gloucester, England. Fred West was arrested in 1994 and charged with 12 murders, while Rose West was charged with 10 murders. Fred West committed suicide in his prison cell in 1995, before his trial could take place. Rose West was found guilty of 10 murders and sentenced to life in prison. She is still there.

Ian Brady and Myra Hindley were a British couple convicted of the murders of five children in the 1960s. The victims were all aged between 10 and 17, and were sexually assaulted before being murdered. The bodies of four of the victims were found buried on Saddleworth Moor, near Manchester, England. Hindley and Brady were arrested in 1965, and both were found guilty of three of the murders. They were both sentenced to life in prison. Hindley later admitted her involvement in all of the murders. Hindley died in prison in 2002. Brady died at a secure psychiatric unit in Ashworth Hospital in 2017.

Which serial killer killed the most people? That is difficult to answer, as many do not disclose details of all their victims, but among some of the most prolific must be:

Dr Harold Shipman, with 218 probable murders and possibly as many as 250. However, he was actually only convicted on a sample of 15 murders.

Luis Garavito was believed to have murdered over 300 people (mostly children). He was convicted of over 190 murders in Columbia and neighbouring countries between October 1992 and April 1999. Originally he was sentenced to over 1000 years imprisonment, but may now be eligible for parole.

Pedro López was also believed to have murdered over 300 people, mostly young girls, in Peru and Ecuador between 1969 to 1980. He was convicted of 3 murders in 1983 but claimed to have killed several hundred. Despite this, he was released from a Columbian prison in the late 1990s. His current whereabouts are unknown.

The youngest serial killer is thought to be Amarjeet Sada from India. He committed his first murder when he was only 8 years old, and killed three children, including his own sister who was 8 months old. Amarjeet was born in 1998 to a poor family in Bihar, India. His father was a labourer. In 2006 Amarjeet murdered his 6 month old cousin, the daughter of a maternal uncle. Shortly after, he murdered his own sister. While Amarjeet's family and some villagers were aware of the child's involvement in these two murders, they were considered "family matters" and went unreported. In 2007 Amarjeet killed again, this time a neighbour's 6-month-old daughter named Kushboo. He happily confessed to killing the baby and took villagers to where he had partly hidden her body. It is likely Amajeet was found guilty of murder, but at such a young age would have been tried as a juvenile. In Indian law, he could not have been imprisoned any more than three years. Due to his mental state at the time the crimes took place, it is possible he served his sentence in a psychiatric institute. Little is known about what has happened to him, but it is likely he is now a free man.

How have serial killers hidden or disposed of victim's bodies? Several different methods have been used, including burial, hiding them behind false walls and under floorboards, cutting up and disposing in drains, burning, and dumping in remote areas. The 'Acid Bath Murderer', John Haigh, was a British serial killer who murdered six people between 1944 and 1949. He would lure his victims to his workshop and kill them by hitting them on the head with a mallet. Then he'd dissolve the bodies in a bath of sulfuric acid, in order to get rid of the evidence. He was arrested in 1949 and confessed to the murders, but pleaded insanity. This was not accepted and he was found guilty and sentenced to death. He was hanged in 1949.

GANGSTERS

Defined as notorious violent criminals, some infamous gangsters are detailed below:
     Al Capone, also known as "Scarface," was a notorious American gangster during the Prohibition

era. He rose to power as the leader of the Chicago Outfit, a criminal organization involved in bootlegging, extortion, and other illegal activities. Capone was eventually convicted of tax evasion and served 11 years in prison.

John Dillinger was an American gangster during the Great Depression, and known for his string of bank robberies and prison escapes. He led the Dillinger Gang, which was responsible for several high-profile crimes. He was eventually killed by FBI agents in 1934.

Bonnie and Clyde (Bonnie Parker and Clyde Barrow),were a notorious criminal couple who operated in the central United States during the Great Depression. They were known for their string of robberies, mostly of small banks and stores. They were killed by police officers in 1934.

Pablo Escobar was a Colombian drug lord and leader of the Medellín Cartel, one of the most powerful criminal organisations in the world. He was responsible for the distribution of huge amounts of cocaine and considered one of the wealthiest and most powerful criminals of all time. He was killed by Colombian police in 1993.

James 'Whitey' Bulger was an American gangster and crime boss from South Boston, Massachusetts. He led the Winter Hill Gang and was involved in a wide range of criminal activities, including extortion, money laundering, and murder. Bulger was on the run for 16 years before being captured in 2011, and was sentenced to life in prison in 2013. He died in October 2018.

The Kray twins, Ronald and Reginald, were English gangsters who were active in the East End of London during the 1950s and 1960s. They were known for their involvement in organised crime, including extortion, racketeering, and murder. The Kray twins were both charismatic and violent, and they controlled a large criminal empire that included nightclubs, gambling dens, and protection rackets. They were eventually arrested and convicted of murder in 1969 and sentenced to life in prison. Both are now dead. They are considered to be among the most notorious criminals in British history.

Unexplained mysteries.

We are all intrigued by unexplained mysteries. They remind us of the limits of our understanding and knowledge; the vastness of the unknown. They leave us with more questions than answers, and force us to confront our own ignorance and vulnerability. They make us wonder if there is more to this world than what we know. But perhaps the most worrying thing about unexplained mysteries is that they may never truly be solved… we can only wonder. The world is a mysterious place, and there are some things that will always remain beyond our understanding…

THE MARY CELESTE

What happened on The Mary Celeste is a mystery that has puzzled historians and armchair detectives for decades. It was a merchant ship that set sail in 1872, and was found adrift in the Atlantic Ocean a month later, with not a soul on board. The crew and passengers had vanished without a trace, and the ship itself was in good condition, with no sign of struggle or distress.

To this day, no one knows what happened to the people on board, and the case remains one of the greatest unsolved mysteries in maritime history. There had been ten people on the ship, including the captain (Briggs) and his wife and child. The last log entry on 25th November 1872 placed the ship just a few miles from the Azores. Less than two weeks later, a British ship came across the Mary Celeste, and she was deserted. There was some water in the hold, but not enough to cause panic and the ship was perfectly seaworthy. One of the longboats was missing, so it was thought the ship was abandoned suddenly for an unknown reason. A later investigation of the ship found no evidence that anything untoward had happened.

The ocean holds secrets and mysteries that we may never hope to know or understand, and the reason the crew left the ship – and their fate – will forever remain a mystery.

THE VOYNICH MANUSCRIPT

The Voynich Manuscript is a mystery that has puzzled scholars and cryptographers for centuries. The book, which is believed to have been written in the 15th century, is filled with illustrations and text written in an unknown script that has yet to be deciphered. The book's meaning and purpose remains a mystery, and its pages have been studied by countless experts, including codebreakers from World War II, yet no one has been able to make sense of it.

The book has been carbon-dated to the early 15th century. The script is written from left to right, and the book is divided into several sections, each with its own illustrations and text. The illustrations in the book are also unique, depicting strange plant and astronomical diagrams.

It was purchased by Wilfrid Voynich, an antiquarian book dealer, in 1912. It has been passed down through several owners, including the Beinecke Library at Yale University, which currently holds the book.

Many theories have been proposed to explain the book's meaning, including that it's a hoax, a code, or a form of encrypted language. Some have even suggested that it's written in an extinct language or in a code that's yet to be cracked. However, despite all the efforts, the book's true meaning remains a mystery and a subject of fascination for many people.

THE TUNGUSKA EVENT

The Tunguska Event is a mysterious explosion that occurred in the remote Tunguska region of Siberia, Russia on June 30, 1908. The explosion, which was heard up to 620 miles away, was so powerful that it flattened an estimated 80 million trees over an area of 830 square miles. Despite its devastating impact, no impact crater or debris was found, leading many to believe that the explosion was caused by something other than a meteorite.

Theories range from a meteorite or comet impact, to a natural gas explosion, to a UFO crash, to a black hole passing through the earth.

The explosion was estimated to have been equivalent to a 15-megaton nuclear bomb, and released energy equivalent to around 185 Hiroshima bombs. It caused the sky to light up as far as 1000 km from the explosion site, and caused a seismic shockwave that was recorded as far away as England.

Many scientists have visited the Tunguska site to study the event and try to determine the cause of the explosion, but despite extensive research, the true cause of the Tunguska Event remains a mystery.

THE BERMUDA TRIANGLE

The Bermuda Triangle, also known as the Devil's Triangle, is a region in the western part of the North Atlantic Ocean where a number of ships and planes have vanished without a trace. The area, which is roughly bounded by Miami, Bermuda, and Puerto Rico, has been the site of many mysterious disappearances since the early 20th century. Many theories have been proposed to explain the disappearances, including human error, natural disasters, and even extra-terrestrial activity.

The first recorded incident in the Bermuda Triangle was in 1918, when the USS Cyclops, a Navy cargo ship carrying 309 men, disappeared without a trace.

In 1945, five US Navy Avenger torpedo bombers, known as Flight 19, went missing during a training mission in the area. All 14 crew members were lost and no trace of the planes was ever found.

The SS Marine Sulphur Queen, a cargo ship, went missing in 1963 with 39 crew members on board.

In 1971, a commercial airliner carrying 42 passengers and crew disappeared while flying over the Bermuda Triangle.

The Bermuda triangle was also the area in which the Mary Celeste was found.

Despite the many theories, the true cause of the disappearances in the Bermuda Triangle remains a mystery. Some experts believe that the area's unique combination of ocean currents and unpredictable weather patterns may be responsible for the many shipwrecks and plane crashes that have occurred there. Others, however, continue to believe that there may be a more sinister explanation for the mysterious disappearances. The Bermuda Triangle remains one of the world's most infamous mysteries, and you won't catch me visiting the area, that's for sure.

THE FLANNAN ISLES LIGHTHOUSE KEEPERS

The mysterious disappearance of the Flannan Isles lighthouse keepers occurred in December 1900. The lighthouse was located on the Flannan Isles, which is a group of seven rocky islets in the Outer Hebrides off the west coast of Scotland.

The three lighthouse keepers, Thomas Marshall, James Ducat, and Donald MacArthur, had been on duty at the lighthouse for several weeks and were due to be relieved by a new crew. However, when the relief crew arrived, they found the lighthouse empty. The three keepers had disappeared without a trace, leaving behind no sign of their fate.

The relief crew searched the lighthouse and the surrounding area but found no sign of the missing men. The last entry in the lighthouse logbook was dated December 15th and described severe winds and a storm. But other than an overturned chair, there was nothing untoward to indicate what had happened to the men. Some said that the keepers had fallen victim to the wrath of the sea, their bodies washed away by the storm. But other rumours talked of darker forces at play, of demons and ghosts, otherworldly beings and sea monsters.

We will probably never know the true fate of the Flannan Isles lighthouse keepers. But one thing is certain - their story continues to haunt us as yet another tragic and unexplained mystery.

Is there anyone out there?
(UFOs, Aliens, time travel, other dimensions...)

UFOS AND ALIENS

In the vast expanse of the universe, there may be more than meets the eye. Beyond our world, beyond our solar system, there may be life forms and civilisations we can barely imagine. They may come to us in Unidentified Flying Objects that streak across the sky, defying explanation and arousing our curiosity. This is a look at the possibility of extra-terrestrial life, the history of UFO sightings, and the search for answers in a world full of questions. It is a journey through the unknown, looking at the possibilities of life on other planets. What is the likelihood? What is the evidence? Are supposed sightings of little green men nothing more than weather phenomena or aircraft, or the fevered imaginings of our overactive brains?

The truth of whether they exist or not is out there... somewhere. But will we ever know? In the end, whether they exist or not, the idea of UFOs and aliens is a reminder of the vastness of the universe and the insignificance of our place in it, and that alone is enough to keep us looking up to the skies in wonder and awe.

There have been many official recorded sightings of UFOs and aliens since the early 1900s. The first recorded sighting was in 1900 in Texas, where a group of people saw a large, dark, cigar-shaped object flying in the sky. In 1947, a famous UFO sighting occurred in Roswell, New Mexico, where a flying saucer allegedly crashed, and the US military claimed it was a weather balloon, but conspiracy theories have suggested that it was an alien spacecraft.

The most well-known and controversial UFO sightings of the 20th century occurred in the 1950s and 1960s, with thousands of people reporting sightings of strange, unidentified flying objects in the skies. The Air Force launched Project Blue Book in 1952 to investigate these sightings, and while most were explained as misidentifications of natural phenomena or man-made objects, a small percentage remain unexplained.

There are still reported sightings of UFOs by military personnel, pilots, and civilians, with some countries like France, Chile, and the UK having released their own official reports on UFO sightings.

As recently as 2020 and 2021, there were sightings of UFOs when US Navy aircrafts were chased by unidentified objects which were recorded by the pilots.

Here are a few more details about some famous reported encounters:

The Kelly-Hopkinsville Encounter (1955): In this infamous case, two families in rural Kentucky reported that they were visited by strange, grey aliens with long arms and glowing eyes. The incident lasted for several hours and left the witnesses shaken and terrified.

The Rendlesham Forest Incident (1980): In this well-known case, two US Air Force officers reported encountering a UFO in a forest in England. The officers described a strange craft that seemed to pulse with light, and said that they felt a strong sense of unease while near the craft.

The Phoenix Lights (1997): In this widely-reported case, a series of strange lights were seen over the city of Phoenix, Arizona. Thousands of witnesses reported seeing the lights, which appeared to form a V-shaped pattern and remained visible for several hours.

The Battle of Los Angeles (1942): During World War II, the city of Los Angeles was plunged into darkness after an air raid blackout was declared. However, what followed was a mysterious attack involving bright lights and anti-aircraft fire, leading many to speculate that it was an encounter with aliens.

The Travis Walton UFO Abduction (1975): In this well-known case, a logger in Arizona claimed to have been abducted by aliens after encountering a strange craft in the forest. The man disappeared for several days, and when he reappeared, he claimed to have experienced a series of bizarre and unsettling events while in the aliens' custody.

While many of these sightings can be explained as misidentifications or hoaxes, the fact remains that a significant number of recorded UFO sightings remain unexplained to this day, fuelling the ongoing debate about the existence of extra-terrestrial life and their potential interactions with our planet.

When you consider that the observable Universe is estimated to be around 93 billion light-years across and that there are an estimated 2 trillion galaxies in the bit of Universe we can see, it seems to me that alien life must exist somewhere. But will we ever see or meet them? Well, that's a totally different question.

TIME TRAVEL

Time travel, a thrilling concept of science fiction, has always been fascinating. The idea of being able to slip through the veil of time, to see the past, and possibly change the future, is an exciting thought. Is it just the stuff of science fiction and vivid imagination? Or could it be possible?

Time travel refers to the hypothetical concept of moving from one point in time to another. The idea of time travel has been popularised in science fiction and has been a subject of interest in the fields of physics, philosophy, and mathematics.

One of the earliest theories of time travel was developed by the mathematician and logician Kurt Gödel in 1949. Gödel proposed that time travel is possible in a universe that follows the laws of general relativity, as described by Albert Einstein.

So, the theory suggests that time travel is possible, but it would require a large amount of energy and the manipulation of a massive object, such as a black hole. The theory of quantum mechanics also suggests that time travel is possible, but it would involve the manipulation of subatomic particles. Some scientists suggest that time travel is possible through the use of wormholes, which are hypothetical shortcuts through space-time. However, their existence is unproven.

The "grandfather paradox" is a popular thought experiment that raises questions about the potential consequences of time travel. Many scientists and philosophers have argued that the idea of time travel is inherently paradoxical, as it raises questions about causality and the consistency of the past. For example, if a person were to travel back in time and change the course of history, what would be the consequences for the present and the future?

With our current understanding of physics, time travel is unfortunately not possible at present. We will have to make do, (for the moment, anyway) with watching 'Doctor Who' or reading 'The Time Machine' by H. G. Wells.

Despite the challenges posed by the concept and paradoxes of time travel, the thought continues to captivate the imagination and spark scientific inquiry. Researchers continue to explore the possibilities and limitations of time travel, and many believe that a deeper understanding of the nature of time may, one day, make time travel a reality.

PARALLEL UNIVERSES, OTHER DIMENSIONS, AND ALTERNATE REALITIES.

What if there were doors to other worlds waiting to be opened, if only we had the key? What if we could explore worlds beyond our own?

The concept of other dimensions refers to the idea that there may exist additional dimensions beyond the dimensions of space and time that we experience in our everyday lives. The idea of other dimensions has its roots in mathematics and physics, and has been a subject of interest in these fields for many years.

In physics, the most well-known theory proposing the existence of other dimensions is the string theory, which suggests that the universe has ten or more dimensions, with the additional dimensions being curled up or hidden from view.

Another popular theory proposing the existence of other dimensions is the idea of parallel universes or the 'many-worlds' explanation of quantum mechanics. This theory suggests that there may be an infinite number of parallel universes existing simultaneously with our own, each with its own unique set of physical laws and reality.

The idea of other dimensions has been a central theme in science fiction/fantasy novels and films. Some of note are:

'The Chronicles of Narnia' by C.S. Lewis: This classic series of children's books features a magical world of talking animals and mythical creatures that can be reached through a wardrobe. The Narnian world is depicted as a parallel universe that exists alongside our own, and is a recurring theme in the books.

'Sliders' (TV series): This popular TV series features a group of characters who travel between parallel universes, encountering alternate versions of themselves and different realities. The show was praised for its imaginative take on the concept of parallel universes and other dimensions.

'The Matrix' (film): This ground-breaking sci-fi film features a dystopian world where humans live inside a simulated reality created by sentient machines. The Matrix explores the idea of a parallel reality and the possibility of multiple dimensions existing simultaneously with our own.

'Doctor Strange' (film): This film is based on the Marvel Comics character of the same name, and features a sorcerer who travels to alternate dimensions and parallel realities in order to protect the world. The film features imaginative and visually stunning depictions of other dimensions.

While the existence of other dimensions is still purely speculative, many physicists and mathematicians continue to explore the concept through mathematical and theoretical models. The possibility of other dimensions has far-reaching implications for our understanding of the universe and the nature of reality, and is a subject of ongoing research and discussion.

I'm off to check whether there's a door in the back of my wardrobe.

The terrible and strange things we do – to ourselves and each other.

(Torture, Foot binding, shrunken heads, cannibalism...)

There is a shadow that haunts the human soul, a darkness that lurks within us all. It is a place of twisted desires and grotesque and unnatural acts. It is a realm where the boundaries of normalcy are stretched to their limits and beyond, where people inflict pain and suffering upon themselves and others in the pursuit of pleasure, power, or simple survival.

For some, these acts are driven by cultural tradition or superstition, a belief in the power of the strange and macabre. For others, they are born of desperation, a last-ditch effort to survive in the face of impossible odds. And for still others, they are the manifestation of a twisted and perverted desire, a lust for something darker and more taboo, or a display of pure evil.

These are the stories of some of the weird things people do to themselves and each other – alive and dead – and a glimpse into the dark side of the human soul.

HISTORICAL TORTURE

Torture has been practised for centuries around the world, but is now widely recognised as a gross violation of human rights. In recent history, the outlaw of torture has been formalised in different international and national laws.

One of the most famous places in England where torture was carried out was The Tower of London, now a popular tourist attraction. It is a historic castle and prison in the heart of London, and has a long and notorious history of using torture as a method of interrogation and punishment. During the medieval and early modern periods, various forms of torture were used there such as:

The Rack: a device consisting of a wooden frame with rollers at one end, used to stretch the limbs of prisoners.

The Scavenger's Daughter: a form of the rack where the victim was placed in a metal frame that compressed their body.

The Iron Maiden: a cabinet-like structure with sharp metal spikes inside, used to impale or crush the prisoner.

The Judas Cradle: a pyramid-shaped seat with a pointed tip, on which prisoners were forced to sit for hours or even days.

The Spanish Boot: an iron boot that was tightened around the leg of the prisoner, crushing their bones.

The Water Torture: a method of using water to simulate drowning, which was used to extract confessions or information from prisoners.

The Manacles: heavy iron shackles used to immobilise prisoners and cause pain and discomfort.

The Scold's Bridle: a metal cage placed over the head, which was locked around the prisoner's jaw and face and was used to silence women accused of gossiping or being a "scold".

The Tower of London held a wide variety of prisoners, including political prisoners, religious dissenters, and common criminals. Some were subjected to various forms of torture. In addition to physical methods of torture, some prisoners were unlucky enough to suffer psychological forms of abuse such as isolation, humiliation, and threats of execution.

The Tower of London was used as a prison for both short-term and long-term detainees, and some prisoners were held there for many years. Some high-profile prisoners held at the Tower included members of the royal family, nobility, and politicians. The use of torture was generally carried out by 'professional torturers', who were employed by the government and paid for their services.

Some replicas of the equipment used for torture in the past is on display at the Tower, including: The Rack, The Scavenger's Daughter, The Iron Maiden, The Manacle and The Scold's Bridle.

There are many incidences of known torture throughout history that people will never forget. Thankfully, people today are not generally tortured. It was officially banned in England in the 17th century, after the signing of the English Bill of Rights in 1689, which stated that "excessive bail ought not to be required, nor excessive fines imposed; nor cruel and unusual punishments inflicted." However, the use of torture had been in decline for some time before that. It was gradually phased out in England and by the 18th century, it had largely fallen out of use. The last recorded use of torture in England was in the 17th century.

The United Nations 'Convention Against Torture and Other Cruel, Inhuman or Degrading Treatment or Punishment' was adopted by the UN General Assembly in 1984 and came into force in 1987. It defines torture as "any act by which severe pain or suffering, whether physical or mental, is intentionally inflicted on a person for such purposes as obtaining from him or a third person information or a confession, punishing him for an act he or a third person has committed or is suspected of having committed, or intimidating or coercing him or a third person, or for any reason based on discrimination of any kind."

The International Covenant on Civil and Political Rights (ICCPR) adopted by the UN General Assembly in 1966, also prohibits torture. In many countries, the use of torture is specifically prohibited by national laws, and those who engage in torture can be prosecuted under criminal laws.

However, torture still continues to occur in some countries, often in secret and in violation of the law. The international community and human rights organisations continue to work towards the universal abolition of torture.

BODY MODIFICATION

Body Modification is a wide-ranging practice that involves altering the body in some way, often for the purpose of self-expression or as a symbol of cultural or personal identity. Some examples of body modification include piercing and tattooing. While some people view these practices as a form of self-expression and consider them to be 'main stream', others may see them as a way to inflict pain and suffering on themselves or others. Tattooing, for example, involves the insertion of ink into the skin using needles, which can cause significant discomfort and pain. Piercing often involves the insertion of jewellery into the skin, which can cause infection and other health problems if not done properly. Scarification involves the creation of scars on the skin, which can be painful and take a long time to heal. These practices can be risky and may have long-term health implications.

Neck elongation is a practice still observed today in some cultures, where women wear heavy rings or other forms of jewellery around their neck in order to stretch it over time. The idea behind this is to create an illusion of a longer neck, which is seen as a symbol of beauty and status. The heavy jewellery can cause significant discomfort and neck pain, and can cause damage to the spinal column and surrounding muscles. In some cases, the neck can become so elongated that it can no longer support the weight of the head, leading to a lifetime of physical pain and disability.

Chinese Foot-Binding was an ancient practice first introduced in the 10th century and continued until the early 20th century. It involved binding the feet of young girls so that they would remain small and dainty, which was considered a symbol of beauty and wealth. The bindings were often so tight that they caused permanent deformation, leading to lifelong pain and mobility issues. The practice was seen as a rite of passage for young girls, who would often be forced to undergo the procedure without any pain relief or anaesthesia. Sometimes the bindings were so tight that girls were unable to walk or care for themselves.

The girl's feet were first soaked in warm water with herbs and animal blood. This helped to soften them and make them easier to bind. The

smaller four toes were then curled over to the sole of
the foot with significant force. Binding cloths were
used to bend the toes underneath the sole. At the
beginning, feet were tightly bound to get them used
to the binding, then they would be bound tighter and
tighter later on. This process lasted for several days to
two months. The toes and arch were then forcefully
broken, and binding cloths were used to curl and hold
the feet further. Feet were tightened this way until
they no longer grew.

Foot binding was finally made illegal in
1912. Attitudes changed, but some people still bound
their feet secretly, mostly in poor villages. Foot
binding was completely abolished in 1949, and today's
women don't bind their feet.

SHRUNKEN HEADS

The practice of shrinking heads, or 'Tsantsa' as the
indigenous people of South America knew it, dates
back centuries and was practiced by the Jivaro tribes
of Ecuador and Peru. Heads were shrunk as part of a
ritual to honour the dead, and were believed to hold
the power and strength of the deceased. Some tribes
shrunk the heads of their enemies, and sewed up the
eyes and mouth to trap the spirit. The process
involved removing the skull, boiling the skin and
flesh, and then moulding it into a smaller size (about
one third) using pebbles and string. They then used
the finished product as a talisman, trophy, or as a
symbol of power in warfare and hunting.

Head shrinking fell into decline in the 20th
century as a result of pressure from Western
colonisers and Christian missionaries. In the late 19th
century, shrunken heads became popular as curiosities

and souvenirs. As a result, the practice of head shrinking was banned, and today it is illegal to buy or sell shrunken heads. However, they are still highly sought after by collectors and museums, and remain a powerful symbol of the cultural and spiritual beliefs of the indigenous people of South America. Whether viewed as a gruesome reminder of the past or as an important part of cultural heritage, shrunken heads remain a fascinating aspect of human history.

CANNIBALISM

Cannibalism is the act of consuming the flesh or organs of another human being. It has been recorded throughout history and across cultures. From the ancient civilisations of the Aztecs, to more recent examples like the Donner Party in 19th century America, cannibalism has been a brutal and gruesome aspect of human behaviour. In many cases, it has been driven by necessity, such as in times of extreme hunger or famine, but in others, for religious or cultural practices.

Sometimes, cannibalism is driven by psychological factors, such as mental illness or disorders. Some cases of cannibalism have been linked to psychopathic or sadistic tendencies. Despite being widely condemned, cannibalism continues to occur in various forms around the world. In recent years, there have been numerous cases of people being charged with cannibalism, including a German man who was found to have stored human flesh in his refrigerator, and an Austrian man who killed and ate a man he met online. These cases serve as a grim reminder of the horrific things that people are capable of doing to one another. Whether driven by necessity, psychology, or pure evil, cannibalism remains a shocking act.

CRYONICS

Cryonics is the low-temperature preservation of a human body with the hope that medical technology will advance to a point where the individual can be revived and restored to health. This is typically done by freezing the body in liquid nitrogen at a temperature of around -196°C.

The theory is that at low temperatures, the body's metabolism slows down, and the damage caused by disease and death can be minimised. The hope is that future medical technology will be able to repair or reverse the damage, and bring the individual back to life.

Cryonics is a controversial and unproven field, and there is currently no scientific evidence to support the idea that a frozen body can be successfully revived. Nevertheless, there are several organisations around the world that offer cryonic preservation services. It is estimated that there are currently around 350 people who have been cryopreserved worldwide, with the majority of them being in the United States.

I do hope they haven't got freezer burn.

Against all odds.
(Survival in the face of terrible adversity).

In this chapter, we'll delve into the incredible stories of human survival in the face of adversity. Fiendish things can happen to any one of us, as the incidents below show. One day you're walking along, minding your own business, the next you've fallen thousands of feet out of a plane; been struck by lightning; or become lost in a desert…

When challenging things happen, how we deal with it *matters*. If you have the right frame of mind and strength of will, courage and determination, it seems the human spirit can triumph and survive despite terrifying circumstances – even when the odds are stacked against you. Here are some amazing examples.

Aron Ralston is a mountaineer, engineer, and motivational speaker who gained fame for his harrowing experience while hiking in Blue John Canyon, Utah, in April 2003. While exploring a narrow slot canyon, a boulder shifted and trapped Ralston's right arm against the canyon wall. Despite attempting to free himself for several hours, he realised he was stuck and that his only hope of survival was to amputate his arm.

Ralston had no mobile phone signal, and he had not told anyone where he was going, so he knew that no one was coming to rescue him. He spent the next five days trapped in the canyon with little food or water, as he had only a small amount of water and some snacks with him.

On the fourth day of his ordeal, Ralston realised that he had to take drastic measures to free himself. Using a dull multi-tool, he amputated his own arm just below the elbow. After freeing himself, he had to rappel down a 65-foot cliff and hike out of the canyon for several miles before he was finally rescued.

Ralston's story became the basis for the movie "127 Hours," directed by Danny Boyle and starring James Franco as Ralston. The film was nominated for six Academy Awards, including Best Picture, and won an Oscar for Best Original Song.

After his ordeal, Ralston became an advocate for wilderness safety and the importance of leaving detailed plans with someone before heading into the wilderness. He also continues to be an active adventurer, having climbed all 59 of Colorado's 14,000-foot peaks and completed the Leadville Trail 100, a 100-mile ultramarathon. Wow!

Juliane Koepcke is a German-Peruvian biologist who is known for surviving a plane crash in the Peruvian rainforest in 1971 when she was just 17 years old. Juliane and her mother were flying to Pucallpa, a city in eastern Peru, to visit her father, who worked there. The flight was on Christmas Eve and it was on a LANSA Flight 508.

While flying over the Amazon rainforest, the plane was struck by lightning and broke up in mid-air. Juliane, who was seated in the rear of the plane, was sucked out of the fuselage and fell two miles to the ground, still strapped to her seat.

Amazingly, she survived the fall and woke up the next morning still strapped to her seat, with a broken collarbone, a deep cut on her arm, and her right eye swollen shut. She found a bag of candy nearby and used it as her only source of food for the next few days.

After the crash, Juliane embarked on a harrowing 10-day trek through the jungle, wading through waist-deep water and fighting off swarms of insects. She eventually found a small stream and followed it downstream, hoping to find help.

On the 10th day, Juliane stumbled upon a group of loggers who took her to a nearby village, where she was able to receive medical treatment. She later discovered that she was the only survivor of the 92 people on board the plane, including her mother.

Juliane's incredible story of survival has been the subject of several books and documentaries. She went on to become a biologist and has dedicated her life to studying the rainforest and advocating for its preservation.

Roy Sullivan was a park ranger who lived in Virginia, USA, and was known for surviving seven different lightning strikes, earning him the nickname "the human lightning rod". Sullivan was born in 1912 and worked as a park ranger in Shenandoah National Park for more than 35 years.

Sullivan's first lightning strike occurred in 1942, when he was standing in a lookout tower and a bolt of lightning hit the tower, knocking him unconscious. After that, he was struck by lightning six more times, with the last strike occurring in 1977, when he was 65 years old.

Sullivan's most famous strike occurred in 1969, when he was hit by lightning while inside his truck. The bolt of lightning travelled through the truck's window and hit Sullivan directly in the head, setting his hair on fire. Despite suffering burns and hearing loss, Sullivan managed to drive himself to a nearby ranger station for treatment.

Sullivan's incredible survival earned him a place in the Guinness Book of World Records for "most lightning strikes survived". However, his experiences also took a toll on him, and he developed a fear of thunderstorms later in life. Sadly, he passed away in 1983 at the age of 71 from a self-inflicted gunshot wound. His death was not related to any of his lightning strikes but was reportedly due to personal issues he was struggling with at the time.

Roy Sullivan's life and experiences have inspired many, and he serves as a reminder of the power and unpredictability of nature.

Mauro Prosperi is an Italian police officer and ultramarathon runner who participated in the 1994 Marathon des Sables, a six-day, 233-kilometre race through the Sahara Desert in Morocco. During the fourth stage of the race, a sandstorm hit the area, causing Prosperi to lose his way and become disoriented. He wandered in the desert for days, trying to find his way back to civilization.

Prosperi had limited supplies with him, including water and food, which quickly ran out. He was forced to drink his own urine and eat bats, snakes, and scorpions to survive. He also used his compass to navigate and followed a trail of ants to find water.

After nine days, Prosperi was found by a nomadic family who gave him shelter and water. They contacted the race organizers, who sent a helicopter to rescue him. He was flown to a hospital in Algeria, where he was treated for dehydration, malnutrition, and sunstroke.

Despite his ordeal, Prosperi made a full recovery and returned to running. He went on to compete in several more ultramarathons, including the Marathon des Sables, which he completed in 2007.

Prosperi's story of survival in the Sahara Desert has become legendary, and he has been praised for his strength, endurance, and determination.

Harrison Okene is a Nigerian cook who was working on a ship, the Jascon-4, when it capsized and sank off the coast of Nigeria on May 26, 2013. The ship was carrying out maintenance work on an oil platform when it overturned in rough seas, trapping Okene and 11 other crew members inside.

As the ship sank, Okene managed to find an air pocket in the overturned vessel, which became his only source of oxygen. He spent the next three days trapped in the cold, dark, and narrow space, with no food or water, fearing for his life.

The situation looked bleak until a team of divers who were working on the salvage of the ship discovered Okene alive in the air pocket. They managed to communicate with him and provide him with food, water, and oxygen. The divers also used hot water to warm him up and prevent hypothermia.

The rescue operation was difficult and dangerous, as the divers had to navigate through the debris-filled water and the ship's narrow passageways to reach Okene. They had to use cutting tools to create a hole in the ship's hull and pull him out.

After being rescued, Okene was taken to a decompression chamber to help his body adjust to the sudden change in pressure. Despite the ordeal, he survived and was reunited with his family.

Okene's incredible story of survival has been widely covered in the media, and he has been hailed as a miracle survivor.

Sir Ernest Shackleton and his British crew's incredible survival story is a testament to human endurance, resilience, and leadership. Shackleton led a team of 28 men on an expedition to cross the Antarctic continent in 1914 on board the ship, Endurance. However, the ship became trapped in ice and was eventually crushed, leaving the crew stranded on the ice.

Shackleton's leadership was pivotal in ensuring the survival of his men. He recognised the seriousness of the situation and kept his crew's morale high. He kept them busy and engaged in daily activities, which helped them to maintain a sense of purpose and hope. When the ice began to break up, Shackleton led his men on a perilous journey on foot across the unstable ice to reach an uninhabited island.

The journey was gruelling, and the crew faced extreme weather conditions, hunger, and exhaustion. They were forced to drag their boats across the ice, and the journey took several weeks. However, they finally reached the island, where Shackleton refused to give up on his crew. He led a small team of men on a dangerous journey in a small boat to reach a whaling station on South Georgia Island, where they could call for help. The journey was fraught with danger, but after several attempts, they finally succeeded in reaching the whaling station and organising a rescue mission.

Thanks to Shackleton's leadership and the determination of his crew, all 28 men survived their ordeal. They had endured two years of extreme hardship, but their courage, resourcefulness, and resilience ensured their survival against incredible odds.

Viktor Frankl was an Austrian neurologist and psychiatrist who is known for his remarkable survival story as a prisoner in Nazi concentration camps during World War II. Frankl was imprisoned in four different camps, including Auschwitz, and was subjected to extreme physical and mental torture.

Despite the horrific conditions and the constant threat of death, Frankl refused to give up hope. He found purpose and meaning in his experiences by observing and studying the behaviour of his fellow prisoners. He realised that those who had a sense of purpose and meaning in their lives were more likely to survive, while those who had lost hope and given up on life were more likely to die.

Frankl's observations led him to develop his theory of logotherapy, which emphasises the importance of finding meaning and purpose in life. He believed that humans have a fundamental need for meaning and purpose, and that this need is the key to mental health and well-being.

After his release from the concentration camps, Frankl continued to develop his ideas and became a renowned psychotherapist and author. His most famous book, "Man's Search for Meaning," is a powerful memoir of his experiences in the camps and an exploration of his theory of logotherapy.

Frankl's work has had a profound impact on the field of psychology and has inspired countless people to find meaning in their lives, even in the face of adversity. His work continues to inspire people around the world to live more meaningful and fulfilling lives.

Hopefully, none of us will face any of the harrowing circumstances these people did. But if you do – remember, they triumphed against all odds. With luck on your side and the right attitude, so can you.

Vivid Imaginings—or are they?
(Stories, books and films.)

The human imagination is vast and spectacular. As Albert Einstein said, 'Imagination is more important than knowledge. Knowledge is limited. Imagination encircles the world.'

We have many uses for our imagination — but some writers certainly use it to dream up fiendish things for stories, books and films. The imagination can even fuel stories of legends, myths, and monsters.

As already discussed, the dark side, the unexplained, and the fiendish fascinate many of us; including documentary writers, filmmakers, and authors.

Below I discuss why we love horror books and films, and look at some of the best and infamous. But not to worry, they are only the fiendish things from our vivid imaginings. Or are they? Only you can decide...

So, why do we love horror books and films so much? Perhaps horror stories provide a way to experience the thrills and chills of unknown and scary things from the comfort and safety of our own homes. We get to explore a dark and different world without actually putting ourselves in harm's way.

They may also be an excellent way to release stress and anxiety. When we're scared, our bodies release adrenaline, which can give us a rush of energy and make us feel more alert. This release can feel cathartic – pent-up emotions can dissipate, and we can become so involved in the story that it is a

101

welcome distraction from the stresses of daily life. We can do this without worry because we retain control–we can turn off the movie or close the book if it gets too intense. This feeling of control over the situation can be empowering.

Finally, some people simply enjoy the thrill of being scared. It's a bit like riding a roller coaster - the adrenaline rush can be addictive, and some of us enjoy seeking out that feeling of fear. So, the next time you're settling in to watch a horror movie or read a spooky story, remember that you're not alone in enjoying the feeling of being scared!

Whatever the reason we enjoy them, there have been many influential and iconic horror books and films over the years. Roughly in date order, here are a few scary favourites.

The Pit and the Pendulum (1842 short story, 1961 film adaptation) Written by Edgar Allan Poe, The Pit and the Pendulum is a macabre tale about a man who is sentenced to death during the Spanish Inquisition. As he is locked in a dark dungeon, he begins to experience a series of terrifying and hallucinatory tortures, including a swinging blade known as the pendulum. With its gothic atmosphere and visceral imagery, The Pit and the Pendulum is a haunting story that has inspired countless adaptations and homages in horror media.

Hammer Film Productions was a British film production company that specialized in horror films from the 1950s to the 1970s. The company's first major horror hit was **'The Curse of Frankenstein'** (1957), which starred Peter Cushing as the Baron and Christopher Lee as the creature.

Frankenstein, the monster made from dead people's body parts and brought to life with electricity, was the brainchild of Mary Shelley, an English author. The book was first published in 1818. Since then, Frankenstein has become an iconic monster whose story still manages to shock us, because his creator, Victor, brings him to life in the name of science, with no thought of what the monster will be like or how it will think or feel. When Victor doesn't like his creation, he rejects him. Perhaps there is more than one monster in this book.

The Haunting of Hill House (1959 novel, 1963 film adaptation, 2018 Netflix series) Written by Shirley Jackson, The Haunting of Hill House is a story about four people who spend a summer in a notorious haunted house to study paranormal activity. As they explore the sinister mansion, they begin to experience supernatural phenomena and uncover the tragic history of the house and its former inhabitants. The novel has been adapted multiple times, including a 1963 film directed by Robert Wise and a critically acclaimed 2018 Netflix series created by Mike Flanagan. With its atmospheric prose and intricate characterisations, The Haunting of Hill House is a classic work of horror fiction.

'Psycho' (1960) is a horror film directed and produced by Alfred Hitchcock. Based on the book of the same name and loosely on real-life serial killer Ed Gein, it starred Anthony Perkins as Norman Bates and Janet Leigh as Marion Crane. The shower scene with screeching violins is unforgettable. 'Psycho' is short for 'psychopath' which is used to describe someone who is callous, unemotional, and morally depraved. Usually anti-social, they also lack empathy for others. Many serial killers are psychopaths, and Norman Bates was no exception. 'Psycho' was Hitchcock's most successful film financially, and even though it was made on a low budget and filmed in black and white, it is widely considered a masterpiece of the genre.

'The Birds' (1963 film) again directed by Alfred Hitchcock, is a classic horror film about a small California town that is suddenly besieged by swarms of aggressive birds. As the attacks escalate, a wealthy socialite named Melanie Daniels becomes involved in a dangerous game of cat and mouse with the invaders. With its eerie score, stunning visuals, and Hitchcock's trademark suspenseful storytelling, The Birds is a masterpiece of cinematic horror.

'Rosemary's Baby' (1967 novel, 1968 film adaptation) Written by Ira Levin and directed by Roman Polanski, Rosemary's Baby is a chilling story about a young woman named Rosemary who moves into an apartment building with her husband Guy. After becoming pregnant, Rosemary begins to suspect that her strange neighbours are part of a satanic cult. As her paranoia grows, she becomes increasingly isolated and desperate to protect her baby from their clutches.

'The Exorcist' (1973) directed by William Friedkin, told the story of a young girl possessed by the devil and two Catholic priests' attempt at exorcism. It was based on the best-selling book of the same name by William Blatty. A fire on set and crewmember deaths led to a belief the film was cursed. People flocked to see it at the cinema and it was financially successful despite being banned in some places. It is considered by some to be one of the best horror films ever made. It definitely scared me back in the day.

'The Omen' (1976). Directed by Richard Donner, I still consider this one of the scariest horrors ever made. Starring Gregory Peck, Lee Remick, and Harvey Stephens, it is about a baby being swapped at birth who turns out to be the Antichrist. With a great story and incredibly good acting, the tension builds and builds throughout. Horrifying with a British Gothic feel (it was mainly filmed in England), it's a must-see for all horror fans.

'Halloween' (1978) directed by John Carpenter, tells the story of a mental patient who, at the age of 6, killed his babysitting teenage sister on Halloween. Fifteen years later, he escapes the sanitorium and returns to his home town where he stalks a teenage babysitter (played by Jamie Lee Curtis.). It became one of the most profitable independent films of all time and many sequels were made. It is considered one of the most influential 'slasher' horror films.

'Alien' (1979) directed by Ridley Scott and written by Dan O'Bannon, was a big box office success. A science-fiction/horror film, it is about a spaceship's crew that find themselves up against a terrifying alien. Many sequels were made. The most memorable scene from the film is when the alien bursts from the chest of one of the crew members, and it is considered one of the most iconic scenes from a horror sci-fi film.

'Pet Sematary' (1983 novel, 1989 film adaptation, 2019 film adaptation) Also written by Stephen King, Pet Sematary is a story about a family that moves to rural Maine and discovers a mysterious burial ground behind their house. When their cat is killed, the father, Louis, makes the fateful decision to bury it in the Pet Sematary, not realising the terrible consequences that will follow. As tragedy befalls the family, Louis becomes increasingly desperate to bring his loved ones back from the dead, leading to a horrifying climax that explores the themes of grief, loss, and the dangers of tampering with the natural order.

'IT' (1986 novel, 1990 TV mini-series, 2017 and 2019 film adaptations) another written by Stephen King, is a sprawling epic that spans multiple timelines and follows a group of friends known as the Losers Club, who band together to fight an evil entity that preys on children in the small town of Derry, Maine in the 1950s. The creature, which takes on the form of a clown named Pennywise, is a shape-shifting monster that can exploit the deepest fears of its victims. With themes of trauma, loss, and the power of friendship, IT is a deeply unsettling and poignant horror story.

'Misery' (1987 novel, 1990 film adaptation) again written by King, was directed by Rob Reiner. Misery is a psychological horror story about a famous author named Paul Sheldon who is rescued from a car crash in heavy snow by his biggest fan, Annie Wilkes.

As he recuperates at her secluded home, Paul realises that Annie is not quite what she seems, and her obsession with him becomes increasingly dangerous. With taut suspense and a truly terrifying antagonist, Misery is a masterclass in suspenseful storytelling.

'The Babadook' (2014) Directed by Jennifer Kent, is a psychological horror film about a single mother, Amelia, who struggles to raise her troubled son, Samuel, after the death of her husband. When a mysterious children's book called "The Babadook" appears in their home, they begin to experience supernatural phenomena and their lives spiral into terror. With its striking visuals, haunting soundtrack, and powerful performances by Essie Davis and Noah Wiseman, "The Babadook" has become a modern classic of the horror genre. Don't watch it on your own.

'The Witch' (2015) Written and directed by Robert Eggers, is a supernatural horror film set in colonial New England. The story follows a family who are exiled from their community and forced to live in isolation on the edge of a dark and foreboding forest. As they begin to fall victim to mysterious and malevolent forces, they turn on each other and descend into madness. With its immersive period detail, haunting score, and disturbing imagery, "The Witch" is a chilling exploration of religious hysteria and the darkness that lies within us all.

'Hereditary' (2018) Written and directed by Ari Aster, is a psychological horror film about a family who begins to experience supernatural phenomena after the death of their secretive grandmother. As the mother, played by Toni Collette, delves deeper into the family's dark history, she becomes increasingly isolated and terrified as she uncovers shocking truths about her ancestry. With its harrowing performances and spine-tingling atmosphere, Hereditary has been praised as one of the best horror films of the past decade.

I could go on and on, adding many more fiendish imaginings to this list, but do you really want this book to go on forever…?
Perhaps it's time to read of nicer things.

And wait until take two…

Author's note

Dear reader, I hope you enjoyed this book. Please leave a review on Amazon if you did. If there's anything I've left out that you would like included in a second book, please let me know. (You can contact me by email: sarah@sldavisauthor.com). Remember, it must be *fiendish*.

But please, just remember that when you read books like this, it can seem that the world is a dark, scary and frightening place. Which of course, at times, it can be. But the fact is that good people out-number bad people, and that good things out-number bad things. Now, go and read something warm, soft and fluffy. And when you're ready for some more scary stuff, try my book of short fictional horror stories, 'Twists and Churns' available on Amazon. Only when you're ready, of course...

'Til the next time...
Sarah.
www.sldavisauthor.com

Printed in Great Britain
by Amazon